Jumping through Fires

THE GRIPPING STORY

of ONE MAN'S ESCAPE

from REVOLUTION

to REDEMPTION

DAVID NASSER

BakerBooks
a division of Baker Publishing Group
Grand Rapids, Michigan

Published by Baker Books
a division of Baker Publishing Group
P.O. Box 6287, Grand Rapids, MI 49516-6287
www.bakerbooks.com

Printed in the United States of America

Library of Congress Cataloging-in-Publication Data
Nasser, David, 1970–
    Jumping through fires : the gripping story of one man's escape from revolution to redemption / David Nasser.
        p.   cm.
    ISBN 978-0-8010-1335-5 (cloth)
    ISBN 978-0-8010-7259-8 (ITPE)
    1. Nasser, David, 1970– 2. Christian converts from Islam—Iran—Biography.
3. Conversion—Christianity. I. Title.
BV2626.4.N37A3 2009
248.2′46092—dc22   2009024230

This book is dedicated to the people of Iran
May the relentless grace of God
cause the greatest revolution of all

CONTENTS

1

THE DAY THAT CHANGED EVERYTHING

The whole world was on fire.

Watching my young son stare wide-eyed into the flames on a cool March evening, I remembered how huge and awesome the same sight seemed to me when I was his age. The whole world looked like one giant inferno. My father stood beside him in the driveway, the light flickering on their faces. Dad is not a tall man, but his military bearing makes him seem taller than he is. When I was my son's age, I thought Dad was a giant. His gray moustache and dark eyes emphasized his Iranian features ("Not Iranian," he would say, "Persian!"). I expect that night reminded him of many others like it when he celebrated a cultural tradition going back more than three thousand years.

"Jump, Rudy! Jump!" Dad said. Rudy wanted to do it, but hesitated and held his hand up, arm extended, fingers outstretched.

"Hold my hand, Papa."

With a wide smile my dad reached down and grabbed his grandson's hand. Another world ago, I held that same hand and jumped over a small bonfire like this one, shouting the same ancient Zoroastrian chant Rudy was now yelling as he leaped into the air: *Sorkhie to az man, zardie man az to.* ("Your redness is mine, my yellowness is yours.") The tradition holds that when you jump through the flames, they burn away all the bad things that have happened during the past year, all the sickness and misfortune, and replace them with good health and the promise of new beginnings.

There are hundreds of Middle Eastern families in Birmingham, but we were probably the only family crazy enough to keep the tradition alive in this part of the world. Each of us wore at least one article of clothing that was red, set up a row of bonfires on our middle-class suburban driveway, and ran toward the flames.

What must the neighbors have thought? "Honey, come look! The Iranians are out on their driveway again. Are they trying to set their kids on fire?" In all the years we've done this, it's a wonder the police or homeland security have yet to be called.

Celebrating *Chaharshambe Suri*, or Red Wednesday, by jumping through fires marks the Persian New Year. It happens the night before the first day of spring on the Western calendar. Around the world, hundreds of millions in the Middle East and elsewhere—Muslims, Jews, Turks, Kurds, and others—light bonfires at dusk and feed them all night, welcoming the new year and celebrating the revival of nature. The next day they dump the ashes in a river or at a crossroads, symbolizing the removal of all the sickness and bad stuff the fire had absorbed from everybody who jumped through it the night before.

Our condensed celebration did not include the usual dancing or fireworks. This was the little league version—the most we could do without frightening the soccer moms who drove by in their minivans. This was an adventure, deeply rooted in heritage. Our festivities were for Rudy and our daughter, Grace, and the rest of the family, even if they didn't think much about what it represented—jumping from the old year into the new.

When you're a child like Rudy, or like I was, you can't see through the flame. You jump on faith that there's something safe and solid on the other side. You jump because others have jumped before you and made it, and, most importantly, you jump holding on to a hand you trust, knowing that as long as you hang on, everything will be all right. That hand has always led you to safety, so it wouldn't possibly lead you to harm now. Watching Rudy and thinking about my own nights of jumping through a row of fires seemed a lot like the trials of revolution, religion, and redemption that I have journeyed through in life. They have all been scary, but in reflection, I see now that I was never alone. Through it all I have always been held.

The story I know best begins in Iran, where my father was an officer in the army of the Shah of Iran (*shah* meaning "king"), and my mother came from a long line of distinguished public officials. That's where I first remember the bonfires—men and women dancing together in the street, a rare sight in Muslim Iran—and my father's warm, calloused hand holding tight to mine as he yelled, "Jump, David! Jump!"

But one day the bonfires of a new year's hope and renewal went out, and the fires of death and destruction ignited.

The consuming flames of a revolution brought an end to many things, including permission for Red Wednesday ceremonies. In 1979 the ceremonies were cancelled by the new regime that had come to power in our country. Although it was a cultural celebration without any religious meaning, the new leaders banned it on religious grounds. Then they systematically set out to destroy everything and everyone that didn't meet their standards of a radical Islamic state.

Including me.

One bright winter day, my sister, Nastaran, and I were chauffeured to school as usual. Instead of going through the regular class schedule, however, all the students were called to an assembly. We left our classrooms and tramped down the hallways to the assembly area. I remember feeling grateful to be out of class. I hoped that whatever we were attending would take as long as it could because the longer the assembly, the less schoolwork we would have to do. So there we stood, the whole student body in uniform, elementary through senior high.

It became apparent this was no ordinary break from class when, as we filed into the assembly area, we saw armed soldiers standing in front of the large auditorium. As soon as we were all in place, one of them yelled *"Attention!"* He reached into his pocket, pulled out a sheet of paper, and read three names aloud. My sister and I were on the list. I knew the other name as well. He was the child of the most influential military officer on our base. His father was a pilot like mine. I hoped our fathers had not been killed in a helicopter accident as we walked to the front.

The soldier who read our names returned the piece of paper to his pocket, and with the same hand pulled his pistol out of the holster. He took a step toward me and leveled the gun at my forehead. All I could see was the underside of his starched shirtsleeve running from wrist to elbow. The pistol hovered inches from my skull, smelling of machine oil and gunpowder. After a couple of seconds, the barrel started to shake. I lifted my eyes and looked into the eyes of the soldier. He looked terrified. I was terrified. Everyone was terrified. The only thing scarier than a man with a gun in his hand is a man who looks unstable enough to use it.

Standing only a few feet away, I heard him whispering prayers from the Qu'ran. And then: "I'm going to end your life, but it's not because of who you are. Or because of who your father is. It is for the sake of Allah."

Suddenly I felt the principal's hands grip my shoulder, pushing me away. She stood between me and the pistol, turning herself into a human barricade. "Do not do this!" she said to the soldier. Her voice was full of authority. "This is not a day for killing children. This is not the day." The pistol went back in its holster. The assembly was dismissed, and as if nothing had happened, the entire student body was sent back to class. Nastaran took my hand, and without permission we ran home as fast as we could.

Out of breath and still too surprised to be in shock, we burst into our house and told my dad what happened. I knew my father would know what to do. He always knew what to do. I had visions of my father tearing into the soldier who dared come against his son. *Oh, if that soldier only knew whose son he messed with.*

As my words tumbled out, tears welled up in Dad's eyes and ran down his cheeks. It was the first time I had ever seen my father cry. I didn't know he could. When I finished, he pulled my sister and me close. He picked us up, put us on his lap, and said quietly, "That man with the gun is not going to hurt you. We're going to escape. We're getting out of Iran."

2

ENDING A LIFE

Up until that moment, being a military brat had always been fun. We were part of a whole community of kids who fell into rank, much like our fathers. Our fathers played real army, and we played pretend army. If your dad was the general, you got to be the general, and if your dad was a lieutenant, you were a lieutenant. That was good for me because my dad was a colonel, a helicopter pilot and trainer, and third in command of the military base. Usually the privilege of my father's rank was the gift that kept on giving, but since the revolution had begun, his high position had nearly cost me my life.

Even as a nine-year-old kid, I knew something unusual had been rumbling around us lately, and my mom and dad had been talking a lot about politics and the government. We had already moved once to a place Dad thought would be safer. My sister and I started riding to school with an armed bodyguard. But until that sobering morning, it hadn't made any real difference to me. The day before, my biggest concern was that my pump was broken and I couldn't put air in my soccer ball. Now, the revolution had arrived, dressed as a soldier who somehow thought killing a nine-year-old boy was an act of worship. Who knew, maybe it was a power play to send a message of what happened to kids whose fathers served the shah. But I thought we were *supposed* to serve the shah. Everything was changing at light speed, and nobody had any idea what the future would look like—assuming there was a future. And as far as I could tell, religion was to blame for it all.

Inside the bubble of a little boy's world, things were suddenly falling apart. Outside the bubble, the crisis had been simmering for years. As in most matters of history, it's all incredibly complicated. But the short of it is that back in 1941, our king, Shah Mohammad Reza Pahlavi, was put in power by the British and the Russians at the beginning of World War II to keep the Iranian oil fields away from Hitler's Germany. Years later, the shah was ousted briefly when the democratically elected prime minister, Mohammed Mosaddeq, nationalized the oil fields, triggering an international trade embargo by angry foreign powers who had developed and had run our oil industry. That's when the CIA and British secret intelligence funded a coup that returned Shah Pahlavi to power, and oil production resumed under foreign control as before. A price tag for a barrel of oil was agreed upon, but to many in Iran, it felt like the West was selling a nation's birthright for pennies. Some believed our king, indebted to those who gave him back his throne, had become a puppet whose strings were pulled by the West.

The shah was especially unpopular with conservative Muslims, who saw his pro-West policies not only as a way to fleece a nation of its oil, but also as a way to spit in the face of Islamic law. Iran was on shaky ground; the gap between rich and poor was getting wider, and the middle class was disappearing. Pahlavi replaced the Islamic calendar with an imperial calendar based on the founding of the Persian Empire. To religious leaders in mosques, this was even more affirmation that something drastic had to be done.

Meanwhile, Ayatollah Khomeini (*ayatollah* meaning "a high-ranking Shiite Muslim religious cleric") was stirring up the people with a message of Islamic fundamentalism. From Iraq, where he lived in exile, he was encouraging revolt against the shah. When the Iranian government arranged to have him kicked out of Iraq, Khomeini moved to Paris and continued the battle from there.

It was the perfect storm. Angry people, a shaky economy, and religious opportunists who were ready for action.

By 1979 the shah had begun to lose all control. On January 16, dying of cancer, he left Iran for what was officially called "an extended vacation" in Egypt, and put the Supreme Military Council and his prime minister, Shapour Bakhtiar, in charge. He secretly asked for asylum in the United States, since he had been a loyal ally for more than thirty years. But fearing reprisals and a loss of oil imports from Iran, the administration of President Jimmy Carter turned him down.

Sixteen days later, on February 1, Ayatollah Khomeini returned to Tehran aboard a chartered airliner from Paris.

We were glued to the television set that day. The announcer was declaring Khomeini's return as a triumphant homecoming, but my mother and father saw it as a nightmare that none of us would be able to wake up from. Delirious citizens flooded the city streets to welcome the ayatollah back. I could sense the intensity pouring out of our thirteen-inch black-and-white TV. There was such a mob to greet him that he couldn't get his car through the crowd, so he traveled into the city by helicopter to make his speech. He was a short man with a perpetual frown, dark eyebrows, and a long white beard framed by a severe black turban. This is what Napoleon would have looked like if his mother had hooked up with a Middle Easterner. I remember thinking how, for someone who was finally returning home, he sure didn't seem happy. Pictures of him were everywhere, posted on walls, held up by the crowds. Tens of thousands of people pressed shoulder to shoulder, hands in the air, chanting and waving their fists in rhythm, shouting, "Allah is great! Allah is great!" And then, over and over,

Independence! Liberty! Islamic Republic!
Independence! Liberty! Islamic Republic!
Independence! Liberty! Islamic Republic!

By now, soldiers loyal to the revolution, along with many others caught up in the emotion of the moment, were tearing down every statue of the shah they could find.

The ayatollah set up headquarters at a school in central Tehran and demanded formation of an Islamic state. This action would make him the top religious leader and the head of state as well. It was a power grab, pure and simple, but Prime Minister Bakhtiar refused to back down at first. Three days later, Khomeini appointed his own prime minister and declared the Provisional Revolutionary Government. Now Iran had two competing governments: the caretaker government of Bakhtiar and his Supreme Military Council empowered by the shah, versus the new revolutionary regime, empowered by the ayatollah.

Who would the people follow? More importantly, who would the army obey? Less than a week later, fighting broke out between the loyalist Immortal Guards and the pro-Khomeini Homafaru of the Iranian Air Force. Khomeini declared *jihad*—holy war—against soldiers who refused to surrender. The Islamic forces started taking over radio and TV stations, police stations, and military posts, and handing out weapons to the public. Bakhtiar went into hiding and later escaped to Paris. Leaders and military officers loyal to the shah started disappearing. The streets were filled with oceans of demonstrators, setting mountains of rubble ablaze.

My whole world was on fire.

On the afternoon of February 11, the Supreme Military Council declared itself neutral in the conflict, and so came the end of the resistance. Khomeini assumed power the next day and declared an Islamic state. Rules were everything, and people who didn't obey them were imprisoned, tortured, or killed. The ayatollah banned alcohol and pop-music broadcasts, shut down dozens of publications, and vowed to rid the nation of non-Muslim influence. "There is no room for play in Islam," he declared. "It is dead serious about everything. We want *mujaheds* [crusaders], not drunken revelers." *Time* magazine described the Islamic coup as a "forced march backward on the treacherous road to an Islamic theocracy" (October 1, 1979).

Khomeini and his council obviously relished their newfound power. When a *New York Times Magazine* interviewer asked him what he thought about the mobs chanting his name and the adoring crowds that followed him everywhere, Khomeini said, "I enjoy it. . . . The people must remain fired up, ready to march and attack again. In addition, this is love, an intelligent love. It is impossible not to enjoy it" (October 7, 1979). Known officers of the shah's army were rounded up faster than ever, tried without defense attorneys, juries, or a chance to defend themselves in court, and executed. The first to go were loyalist generals and senior civilian officials. Somewhere in the middle of all this occurred my involuntary confrontation with a converted soldier. A man who was ready to show his allegiance to the ayatollah one late February morning. His weapon: a gun. His target: me.

Needless to say, our escape could not have happened soon enough. As we thought about what to do and how to do it, time was running out for my father faster than we realized.

In early March, one Sunday morning, soldiers burst into our house and dragged my father away. Dad had too much pride to ask for mercy, but my mother fell to the ground and wrapped her arms around my father's legs. This was why my father was dragged out. He couldn't walk because of a wife who loved him too much to let go of his legs. That image will always be seared into my memory. She was crying, screaming, pleading over and over, "Just kill him quickly! Kill him quickly!" I wondered why she was begging these men to turn her into a widow.

After the intruders left, Mom grabbed my sister's hand and mine and told us to pray that our father would be killed quickly. She looked up toward the ceiling and said, "God, let him die quickly." That's the first memory I have of prayer. I knew that I was supposed to bow my head and close both eyes, but I couldn't.

I didn't want to pray to a god who had sent his religious soldiers to my school to terrorize me, and I hated him even more for taking my father away. I was nine years old, but I had already seen enough to know that I wanted nothing more to do with this god and his holy *jihad*.

After her prayer, Mom began to explain why she wanted a quick death for our father. She revealed that Khomeini's soldiers were taking Dad to a nearby park outside the base. There, military men who were still in allegiance to the shah were publicly humiliated, beaten, and in some instances tortured to death. One man was slowly picked apart, piece by piece. It took them six hours to kill him. "This is why we must ask god for a quick death for your father," she said.

That afternoon, miraculously, my dad came back. The soldiers had taken him to the park to kill him, but one of the men in charge there had served under him. There'd been a time when the soldier's wife was bedridden during a pregnancy. Dad had brought him into his office and said, "I know your wife needs you and I know you don't have any more sick days. But you need to go." He had given the soldier a week with his family that the soldier didn't deserve. Dad didn't remember that specific incident because he did that sort of thing all the time. But this soldier said, "You gave me one week with my family, so I'm going to give you one week with yours." He made the others un-handcuff and release my father. The disorganized and chaotic shift of power allowed for such spontaneous changes of mind. It was unprofessional, but Dad wasn't complaining. Just as abruptly as he had been taken, he was released to go.

When Dad returned home two hours later, he found us sitting right where he left us. He and Mom fell crying into each other's arms, and my sister and I hugged him as if he had been resurrected from the dead. Like any good parent, he seized the moment to teach his children a lesson about how no good gesture will return void. As he told us the story about the man who had given him one more week, he leaned in and whispered.

"We've got a week before they come back," he said. "And when that week's up, we're not going to be here."

3

THE GREAT PRETENDERS

Escaping was no easy task. Military personnel who had served under the shah were not allowed to leave Iran. The civilian airport on the other side of Tehran had gone into lockdown, filled with revolutionary officers whose job it was to stop families like ours from escaping.

With the commercial flight option looking bleak, my parents looked elsewhere. At first Dad wanted to steal a helicopter from the army base and fly us all out of the country. A flight to neighboring Turkey was only a few hours away. He felt sure they would give us asylum. The helicopter would have to be loaded down with canisters for refueling, so absolutely no luggage could be taken. It was a gamble, but Dad felt sure we could pull it off. This was my father, the optimist, who saw the plan of somehow sneaking his family on a chopper, getting past the border, refueling in the middle of a desert, and getting permission to land in Turkey as a no-brainer. My mom, however, wouldn't hear of it. In her opinion, there were too many uncertainties with this plan, and besides, someone could shoot us down. She also didn't want to steal. "How would we get the helicopter back?" she asked. This was my mother. Even in the midst of a life-threatening crisis, she stood stubbornly by her morals. If stealing is wrong, it's wrong no matter what the circumstances.

Finally, after exhausting every possible avenue, my parents hatched a plan. The year before the revolution, Mom had gone to the doctor several times due to concerns about her heart. She had been pregnant with my brother Benjamin at that time, and she wanted to make sure her heart was going to be able to bear the strains of labor. The prognosis was that she was fine—it was nothing life-threatening—but it was enough to give her a convincing medical paper trail. Little did we know that her medical history would be our ticket out. Dad knew her two doctors and felt he could make them an offer they couldn't refuse. They were more than doctors, they were profiteers: men who knew that their position and authority could be a way to make money in times of chaos. They were looking to get rich, and we were looking to get out of there. It was a perfect match. We bribed them with a pile of cash to swap my mother's records and X-rays with those of someone else who had serious heart issues. Yes, the same lady who wouldn't "take a helicopter" was now acting deathly ill. Oh, the sacrifices and compromises a mother makes in order to get her children out of harm's way. Next came the passport switch. Dad had to swap his military passport for a civilian one. He used the papers from the doctor to bluff the passport office into thinking he was a steel industry tycoon with a wife in need of emergency surgery in Europe. He also convinced them that the whole family had to go because his fragile wife wouldn't leave them behind to make the trip. The passport office was not to be bribed, but merely "thanked" with gifts and gratuity for their quick service.

Next came the liquidation of our possessions. Most of what we had was quickly and quietly given away to family. We did however, have a need for as much currency as we could subversively carry. We decided to sell our cars, our home, some leftover possessions; but all of it had to happen on the down-low. Anything that was not given away was for sale. Cash only, of course. And exclusively to buyers who could keep our little secret.

You know the feeling of pity you get for the people whose stuff you rummage through in a garage sale? Looking at a pair of shoes that originally cost a hundred dollars, but now has a piece of masking tape attached with twenty-five cents written on it? That's how it felt. No, we didn't throw a garage sale, but many of the items that my father had payed a premium for were now being virtuality gifted away to strangers. This was more than just our leftover junk; it was our life. From the wedding silver to the chandelier that was imported from France, from my dad's extensive book collection to my sister's brand new bicycle, from the pots and pans that held our favorite meals to the Persian carpets that kept our feet warm. This was the perfect moment to buy the Nasser's microwave—the one we shipped in from America to wow people with its ability to zap a potato in two minutes. Now instead of jealousy, you could come and buy it out of charity and compassion. You could help the Nassers out, paying them cash for the things you couldn't afford at full price.

What I most remember losing were my toys.

"Why are we giving my toys away?" I asked. "You know why," they said. And I did know why. "Why should strange soldiers ransack our home and give your toys to their kids when you can give them to your friends?" I knew little about the political landscape of the revolution. All I knew was that I had a great Lego collection, a Six Million Dollar Man, and plenty of other stuff no one else had because we bought it on our shopping trips to Paris. Giving it up was a very big deal. It represented status, and everything that was familiar, comfortable, and safe. Plus, losing it wasn't fair. I hadn't done anything to deserve having my personal treasures taken away.

For the hundredth time, I asked my parents, "Why do we have to escape? Why are people trying to kill us?"

"It's these religious fanatics, the Ayatollah Khomeini and his followers. They're taking over our country." Religion again. I hated religion. We had to escape from it and get to a safe place.

A childhood friend of my dad's must have overheard one of my rants. Out of kindness, he walked toward me, knelt down, and said, "Man, I really like that jacket," pointing to the one I had in the giveaway pile. "I need some toys, do you have any I can buy?" I knew he didn't have any kids, so what did he need kids' clothes and toys for? "I'll give you one thousand *tomans* for your clothes and your Legos." That was way too much. Much more than it was worth, but my father allowed it. It wasn't the money; this man was helping his friend's son let go of his coveted treasures.

One by one, we watched so much disappear. Traded for a pile of cash.

The Persian currency had to be converted. Some was converted to dollars. By the time the banker was paid off to keep the money conversion hush-hush, we were left with roughly seventy-five thousand dollars in cash. I can still remember seeing the stacks of money on our dining room table.

The rest was converted to gold and silver. My parents went shopping for small, valuable items we could take with us. Yet, at the same time, they couldn't raise suspicions by buying too much expensive stuff. It was a life-or-death balancing act. They bought a lot of gold coins that people traditionally gave as gifts at weddings and other special occasions in Iran, but which had just been outlawed due to a portrait of the shah on one side and the imperial flag on the other. Mom got a huge diamond. Dad bought a really gaudy belt made of alternating white and yellow twenty-four-karat gold links studded with diamonds. Then Dad took my baby brother's diaper bag to a cobbler and had him make a false bottom for it, so we could hide cash and jewels in it. Rest assured, the cobbler was well taken care of for his discretion.

I felt like I was in a movie. My dad requested an armed soldier under his command to escort him everywhere he went. Other soldiers took turns guarding our house all night. They dug a trench in the front yard for protection. Nastaran and I would go out to the trenches and deliver hot tea and sandwiches to these men, partly because they were protecting us, and partly to make sure they didn't suspect anything with all the traffic in and out of our house. I liked these soldiers. They were men my father had hand-selected from his regiment. Men that he knew shared his beliefs about Khomeini. They never discussed such beliefs, but there was a mutual understanding. I wanted to be one of them. "Can I go out to the trench and play with my new friends?" I'd ask my mother. "This is fun!" But the answer was always an emphatic no. Speaking of friends, I noticed certain kids on our street were gone. The alleyway that once hosted a dust bowl of kids chasing after a soccer ball was now quiet. *Where were they?* I wondered. I was afraid to ask.

It wasn't all doom and gloom. To a nine-year-old kid, parts of this had its advantages. My parents didn't care if I stayed up late and wasn't getting my homework done. We still had to go to school, but since it was only a matter of time before we left, academics were the least of our worries. We ate junk food and watched a lot of cartoons. Nothing distracts a kid from imminent death like a steady diet of Kit Kats and *Scooby Doo*.

Mom would give me the same speech every day before we left the house. "You *cannot* tell *anybody* at school that we're leaving." They didn't know whom they could trust. The ayatollah's forces were capturing people and torturing them to get information about their neighbors. Your friends could turn on you at any time. Do you change sides to save your life, or do you go down with the old regime? I didn't know which kids I could talk to. My sister and I couldn't confide in anybody, except for a few old friends who came over to the house with their families. We had become the great pretenders. If only they had given Oscars for best performance in secrecy . . .

I'll never forget the day before we left. I walked through my room, thinking, "This is the last time I'm going to be here." To a stranger, the room might have appeared full, but I knew all the things that were sold and gone. We had left just enough furniture and clothes to give the illusion of normalcy. My room and the rest of our house had become nothing more than a stage, with props to fool the ayatollah's men. I sat down and cried as the realization hit. After a while, I wiped my puffy red eyes, blew my nose, and walked into our living room to say goodbye to our closest friends. Surprisingly, this was not an emotional moment. We all pretended again, planning a future get-together that we knew deep inside would never take place. As far as all my other classmates and neighborhood friends were concerned, I would disappear without a trace. None of us would ever know whether the other was dead or alive.

At last the day had come to put our escape plan into action.

My mom started acting like her heart was really bothering her. She was rushed to the hospital in an ambulance where our two doctors examined her. "This woman needs open-heart surgery immediately," they reported. "We don't have a second to spare. We don't have the technology in Iran for what she needs. She must go to Switzerland. As soon as possible."

It worked; we were allowed to buy round-trip airline tickets. My aunt called our school to get the homework assignments for the following weeks, and Dad arranged for a house sitter. The maid was given a grocery list of all the things we would need in the refrigerator awaiting our return. Mom came home from the hospital to find her children going through the motions. Bags were packed for a two-week stay in Europe. Each of us was allowed one bag. I didn't care about what made it in as much as I wanted very much for one item to be left out. Even in the midst of this terrifying ordeal, I attempted to leave behind what was, in my opinion, the most ridiculous outfit known to humanity, the dreaded lederhosen. In an act of fashion felony, my parents had once bought me and Nastaran each a pair of matching lederhosen—traditional German shorts and hideous suspenders. Think the Von Trapp children in the *Sound of Music*. I was determined that the lederhosen were *not* going to escape with us. Because I had not included them in my collection of clothes to pack, I assumed my distracted parents would forget all about them. I was wrong. Because I had not packed the lederhosen, my mother decided they would be the perfect outfit to wear to the airport the next day. After all, who would be suspicious of two children who looked like life-sized Bavarian salt-and-pepper shakers! Then, as if we were well-rehearsed actors in a play, we all got ready for bed, brushed our teeth, and turned off the lights.

4

AT THE AIRPORT

The airport was typically ten to fifteen minutes away. But gone were the days of anything typical. We couldn't possibly take a taxi, because curious eyes would wonder why we weren't driving ourselves. One of the guards in front of our house took the suitcases from my mom and sister. Everything was put in the trunk, except the diaper bag. The all-important diaper bag. It never left my father's grip.

My mother's eyes were completely bloodshot from a week of tears. Her bouts of sobbing were ripping our hearts out. How was she going to survive being separated from her mother, father, sisters, brother, and the only world she had ever known? Concerned, I escorted her to the front passenger side of the car and opened the door for her. Instead of getting in, however, she knelt down and kissed the earth. Then, as if she was unwilling to let go, she scooped up a handful of the warm black dirt and put it in her pocket. "I want to take Iran with me," she explained softly. I looked up to see the soldier standing and listening. "Mama, you're going to be fine. They have good doctors in Europe." If he only knew.

On the other side of the car, my big sister was busy in her own symbolic gesture of goodbye. Nastaran was uprooting a purple petunia from the flower bed, which lined our driveway, so she could press it in her diary. She was trying to be brave—to be a big girl. But she was only two years older than me, and even my nine-year-old eyes could see she was crumbling on the inside. She was best friends with all of our cousins who lived nearby, and Nastaran could not stand the thought of leaving them behind.

I realized then and there that although for my little brother and me the farewell was limited to friends, family, and fun, for the rest of the Nassers it struck a deeper nerve. It was the loss of a nation and its way of life that they loved with deep patriotism. An Iran that had already disappeared with the shah. He was not coming back, and neither were we.

So with Benjamin securely buckled in his baby seat in the back, and the diaper bag safely between my parents in the front, we pulled out of the driveway.

Heading toward the airport, we saw huge crowds in the street running around aimlessly, chanting, "Death to the shah! Death to the shah!" Graffiti was scribbled all over the place. Our car weaved through the lanes, avoiding the people and lurching around drivers behaving erratically. There were bonfires everywhere. People were restless and edgy, and there wasn't a traffic policeman in sight. Streets all over the city were filled with demonstrators. The country was unraveling.

My father saw this confusion and chaos as a silver lining. He hoped it would give us the cover we needed to sneak out under the revolutionary radar. The fifteen-minute drive took over an hour, but Dad had taken that into consideration. We arrived four hours before our flight was to depart. Getting there before lunch meant that we would probably get searched by a guard who was near the end of his shift. Maybe a hungry and weary man would be less alert. We needed every bit of help we could get.

We pulled into the airport lot and unloaded our very nice car—a Mercedes that my father was meticulous about keeping clean. We normally were not allowed to eat or drink in this prized possession, but now we were abandoning it. I wondered how long it would sit there before somebody stole it or set it on fire. Once the authorities figured out what was up, it wouldn't take long. Mom started in on her speech about keeping our mouths shut again. Nastaran and I had memorized it by then. She made it perfectly clear that everything depended on us getting on that airplane to Zurich.

We got out of the car and headed slowly for the main entrance. Mom had to act sick enough to need emergency treatment, but not too sick to be unable to make the trip. I took my father's hand and felt it shaking. I was scared too.

But even more than being scared, I was excited, because we were getting on a plane. That meant I could drink out of a *can*! In Iran, soft drinks came in bottles and only beer came in cans, but in Europe, soft drinks came in cans. Boys drank out of bottles, men drank out of cans—and I was about to drink like a man. I could hardly wait. A little boy's mind can find great shelter in distractions like these.

Armed soldiers filled every nook and cranny of the airport, striding through the crowd, checking papers, poking through people's belongings. Scared and intimidated, I didn't make a sound. Seeing how nervous the guards were made me nervous too.

Dad leaned toward Mom as we walked and said under his breath, "This is stupid. We should never have tried to get out of here with all these valuables. We're going to get caught, and it isn't worth it. If the soldiers find all that money in the diaper bag, they'll know we are trying to escape and kill us on the spot." They would make an example of us, he went on. They wouldn't just turn us away and allow us to get in our car and go home. The revolutionary guards were killing entire families in order to scare all who dared attempt to leave. As a matter of fact, that fear was their single greatest weapon. That was how they controlled the masses of people. Years later, my father told me that at that moment he regretted putting his family so much at risk. He explained that had he known what it was going to be like at the airport, he would have instead let the soldiers come and execute him, and hoped for the best for his wife and children. He had left too many careless clues behind, had confided in too many people about the escape, and had walked into an airport unprepared to answer possible questions. "Why is your wife wearing a gold belt and a matching bracelet when she is going to a hospital?" In hindsight, I'm thankful Dad didn't over-think it because he might not have gone through with it. Sure, his escape plan was riddled with errors and miscalculations, but someone far greater and wiser was holding Dad through this fiery ordeal.

Checking in was going smoothly. It was uneventful, filled with long lines, forms to fill out, and lots of tipping. Tipping had become the wind that was moving our sailboat smoothly through uncharted waters. We were almost at the end of the final checkpoint when a couple of "unofficial" revolutionaries stopped us and told my dad to open one of the suitcases. They were pointing to my mother's bag. I'm sure my dad was relieved that it wasn't the diaper bag, but what he didn't know at the time was that my mother had packed his military uniform in her bag as a surprise for him. Her intent was to honor him by bringing something with such sentimental meaning along, but if these men exposed Dad as a military man instead of a steel industry tycoon, things could get bloody really soon.

Dad knew these men were not real airport security, but gypsies who harassed passengers for whatever they could get. Rather than arguing, he dug around in his pockets saying the key might be lost. One of the gypsies pulled out a knife and said, "I can pry it open," and that's when Mom got an idea.

She began breathing heavily and acting sick. Dad, picking up the plot, explained her condition. "Would you be so kind as to go and get my sick bride a cold drink?" my father asked one of the gypsies. He reached in his coat pocket and gave the man a gold coin. "This should cover the cost for a Coca-Cola." Both men stared at the coin, one that could easily buy hundreds of Coca-Colas, and gladly went to fetch a beverage we never received, which was just fine with all of us.

As we shuffled onto the plane, I looked around and wondered if we were the only ones on board who were running for our lives. We sat in a middle row of four seats. Benjamin on Nastaran's lap, sitting next to mom, and then me, followed by my father. We sat there, hand-in-hand, as if we were an unbreakable chain. Everyone was quiet, and everything was calm now. Even Nastaran was all cried out at the moment. I remember thinking how Benjamin was the only one who had not shed one tear during this whole ordeal. He must have been the strongest. A few minutes after the plane took off, the pilot came on the intercom and began to talk in a language I didn't understand—English. "What are they saying, Papa?" "They are saying it's a beautiful day to fly. Perfect visibility and not a cloud in the sky." How ironic. That's the last thing any of us felt in that moment. What lay ahead was a world filled with fog and uncertainty. We knew exactly what we were running from, but we didn't have a clue what awaited us at the end of that five-hour trip. But why was I to worry? I was holding my father's hand, and the stewardess was coming down the aisle with a cart filled with canned drinks.

5

PURGATORY

Switzerland was our purgatory. We knew that Europe was not the place we wanted as a permanent home, but it was better than the hell we had left behind. On the first day, we took our time and got settled in the hotel. It was a fancy Bavarian-style chalet that made me feel a tad better about the ridiculous lederhosen ensemble I was forced to wear. The next week was filled with sightseeing and lots of television-watching in the room. Dad was plotting his next move. One morning, Mom, Benjamin, Nastaran, and I went down to eat breakfast in the hotel restaurant. When Dad came down to join us, our jaws dropped. He was wearing his army uniform, starched and pressed to perfection. I glanced at my mother and saw her looking at Dad as if she were a teenage girl staring into the eyes of a celebrity heartthrob. He still wowed her, even after twelve years of marriage.

Dad explained that he had an appointment with the American embassy and was going to request political asylum. I didn't know what that meant, but judging from the excitement in his voice, I knew this could result in good news. "When can we go to America?" my mom asked. "Soon, I hope," Dad said. "Very soon."

Three months later we were still in Zurich.

Purgatory was getting old. To put it simply, we were from the wrong place, trying to get into the wrong country, at the wrong time. Since we had landed in Switzerland, relations between Iran and the United States had gone from bad to horrific.

In the States, President Carter's already-low approval rating was heading further south on account of his support of the shah, and politically, things were falling apart for his administration. Carter had already refused the shah entry to America, and we were much, much further down the totem pole. We were denied not once, not twice, but numerous times.

Dad, fortunately, was not the kind of man who gave up. For him there was no other option than getting to America for a new start. My father had always been pro-U.S. He had taken flight training in the States and knew many American military men personally. He had even risked his life in the very first week of the Iranian Revolution by flying American citizens who were stuck in Iran out to the Turkish border. These service men had been his colleagues. America, he thought, would protect us. Why wouldn't they give us refuge?

A longtime family friend, who was a flight instructor to my dad when he had taken flight training in Killeen, Texas, stepped in. Colonel Charles Colston of the United States Army had become an advocate for the Nassers. He offered to be our American sponsor. His friendship with my father represented the "no man left behind" mentality of a soldier who will not rest until his brother is in safe harbor. Colonel Colston called one afternoon and told Dad he had found a sympathetic ear at the American embassy in Munich, Germany. Also, after pulling a few strings, he had managed to enroll my sister and me in the Munich American army base elementary school. This way we could begin to learn English and adapt to an American way of life. He told my father that though it was not the States, Germany was certainly a giant step closer. We boarded the next train from Zurich to Munich.

Germany was the land of sauerkraut, gummi bears, bratwurst sausages, and yes, more of that awful lederhosen. Our days in Germany were bittersweet. While my sister and I enjoyed the bratwurst and gummi bears, our prospects for asylum in the U.S. were about to take a turn for the worse.

At first, the American embassy in Munich was hopeful they could get us passports to America. We heard on the news that the shah was granted access to the United States for cancer treatment. Surely if they are letting him in, we thought, we can't be far behind. But then came news that stopped us in our tracks. On November 4, 1979, two weeks after the shah's entrance into the United States, a mob of Iranian students stormed the American embassy in Tehran and took sixty-six Americans hostage. Eventually, fourteen of them were released, leaving fifty-two in captivity.

The story hit front pages all over the world: "American embassy held hostage by Iran." And here we were, Iranians, going to an American embassy! Rightfully so, America became obsessed with rescuing the hostages. Meanwhile, the American families who were on the military base where we went to school were watching the news every night. As they sat down to dinner each evening, parents and children alike were tuning in to watch the revolutionaries in Iran burn the American flag, gloat about the hostages, and call America the "Great Satan." Not a good time to be from Iran.

The process for getting to America ground to a halt. The embassy told us that no Iranians would be admitted until the hostage crisis was over. Since we were going to be delayed indefinitely, we had to start saving our money. We moved to a smaller apartment and started cutting our spending here and there. No more shopping sprees, no more indulgences. Just the necessities, we were told by Mom and Dad. This, however, never really happened. Dad would tell us we needed to cut corners, and the next day show up at the apartment with flowers for Mom and ice cream for us. I remember specifically going out for schnitzels and radishes at a German fair during the Iranian hostage crises. That night Dad bought a stein of beer that was so large it resembled a keg with a handle. He drank it all. Mom was not happy, but I thought he was a giant! My mother even took us toy shopping at Christmas. I got Legos, of course.

I did not know this then, but some of the frivolous spending was due to my parents trying to keep us distracted from the reality that my mother's heart condition was acting up for real this time. Beware of blinders made of toys and ice cream.

Nine months had passed since we left Iran, and Europe had taken its toll on us. One afternoon, Mom decided she'd had enough. She wrote a letter to the American embassy saying that while Iranians were holding Americans hostage in Tehran, they were holding us Iranians hostage in Germany. Some might say it was my mother's cynical sense of humor in that letter that got the ball rolling again with some high-up bureaucrat in Washington, but I know better. I was there the day she sent it. My mother mailed the letter that day with two carriers. The first was the postal service, the second was a strange prayer. Mom grabbed Nastaran's hand, my hand, and little Benjamin's. "Children, we want to go to America. But I've been thinking, maybe we are praying to the wrong source. Jesus is America's God, not Allah. Maybe we ought to pray to Jesus instead." She then proceeded to ask this Jesus, whose name I had never heard of, to allow us into his country.

Within a week, two huge favors came from the American embassy in Munich. First, they figured out what to do with my brother, Benjamin. Benje has Down syndrome, and we were told that no one with that condition was allowed to receive political asylum. An embassy official re-took his photo so the condition wouldn't be obvious on his application, then let that little detail about him disappear from the forms. The second, bigger problem was that absolutely no Iranians would get asylum in America as long as the hostages were still imprisoned—period. Our friends at the embassy fixed that too, by trading our Iranian passports for German ones. As Germans, we could enter the U.S. immediately without a hitch. It was funny: the only way we could leave Germany was to become German.

Dressed in his military garb one last time, Dad went to the embassy for his final visit. He went to say thank you and to present each of the men who had helped him with a gold coin with the picture of his king. I don't know if they were allowed to take it, but I do know that no one deserved it more.

The next day, as we flew to America, I looked out of the window and prayed with all the sincerity of a nine-year-old, *Jesus, I don't know who you are, but thanks for letting us into your country!*

6

FRUITCAKE

Everything is bigger in Texas. Texas toast is twice as thick as an ordinary slice, and the stars are twice as bright. Texans love to remind outsiders that some ranches in their state are bigger than Rhode Island. I was recently staying at a hotel in Dallas, and the spa in the hotel lobby offered a massage session with four therapists working on you for two hours. The brochure in my room boasted about eight hands working on your back at once. As if getting a massage from one therapist is not indulgent enough. Guess what it was called? "The Eight Hands of Texas Massage."

Texas is as grand as, well, Texas.

Moving to a place like that in the middle of the Iranian crisis was difficult, at best. When we first arrived in the States, my dad's army connections landed us in Killeen, Texas, an hour north of Austin and just outside Fort Hood, the biggest military base in the United States. It was headquarters of the First Cavalry Division, which did a lot of helicopter flying, so my dad hoped he would soon get a job as a flight instructor. My family had lived in America for a year back before I was born while my dad took some specialized flight courses, so it wasn't completely alien territory for us. But this time we were coming in as unemployed refugees with limited resources. Because we had been somewhat living on a budget in Germany, we arrived in the U.S. with some cash and valuables we had held back. We were not part of the "huddled masses" of immigrants with our belongings wrapped in a scarf. Dad was sure the American dream was just around the corner for us. I, on the other hand, wasn't so sure.

Picking out a couch and stocking the cabinets with pots and pans was the easy part of our new American life. The hard part would be school and jobs and friends and all the stuff that really matters. Would we jump through these fires, or right into them?

The place looked and sounded different. I didn't know much English and stuck out like the longest french fry in the bag. I was a wedgie waiting to happen! Nastaran tells a terrifying story about having a knife pulled on her in the school locker room the day we enrolled. She was older, and the stakes were higher for her. My first day in an American school was nowhere near as dramatic. Actually, it must have been downright uneventful, because the only thing I remember is all the blue and white shirts with single stars on them. I didn't know what the star represented, but I knew that if I was going to blend in, I needed my very own star-studded shirt. I took out my Persian-to-English dictionary and looked up the word for star. With broken English, I pointed to a classmate's shirt and asked, "For what is star?" The answer only added to my confusion. "Cowboys!" he shouted. *What does a star have to do with cowboys?*

Eventually I picked up a few more clues and pieced together the connection. The star represented a football team. This was fan gear.

"How was school today?" my mom asked as we arrived home. Nastaran went first and told Mom about her near-death experience. Then it was my turn. "I need a star shirt, please," I pleaded. "I need a shirt with a big star on it." My mother, still in shock over what my sister had said, looked at me, perplexed. "A star? But we're not Jewish."

That was just one example among hundreds of the gaping culture gap I was trying to bridge. Halloween, for example, may be a little scary for those who are familiar with it. Believe me, it is downright terrifying when you're the only student who did not know to dress up for school that day.

In another case of cultural faux pas, I remember standing between two doors trying to decide which one to enter. It was only natural for an Iranian kid who sees "wo" and "men" on a sign to pick it over just "men." That day I learned the hard way that "women" does not mean "big men."

I remember hearing from a classmate about tanning beds. "You mean, you pay to cook your skin?" I asked.

Somehow I got the idea that "Negro" refers to the color black. It didn't go down very well when I shouted that word while pointing to a black cat in the schoolyard.

Then there was the Sears catalog. Suffice it to say that in Iran, it is unthinkable for pictures of women in their undergarments to arrive in the mailbox.

Food was a whole other story. The usual menu back in Iran was grilled kabobs and slowly simmering stews poured over basmati rice. Ours was the land of pomegranates, caviar, rose water, and saffron. For snacks we ate crunchy pistachios, salted cucumbers, fresh dates, and corn grilled over an open fire—not Twinkies and Tang. Now we were in a different world, forced to re-train our taste buds and hungry eyes. I loved the air of mystery as I stood in line at the cafeteria and wondered what could top the sloppy joes, fish sticks, and rectangle-shaped pizzas we were served earlier in the week. It was all a bit overwhelming. Drive-through restaurants. TV dinners. Peanut butter and jelly swirled in the same jar? (How lazy are you people?) Freeze-dried ice cream that astronauts eat? Thirty-one flavors at Baskin Robbins? Back home, if we craved ice cream, it was either vanilla or chocolate. Maybe, just maybe, you'd have the occasional strawberry. Not in America. At Baskin Robbins, you had at least twenty-nine additional choices. And the ice cream truck? Are you kidding me? The ice cream comes to *you*?

America was an impressive place. A land of shopping malls and free samples. I loved this country, but I began to wonder if it loved me back. The harsh reality was that I was different, and different equaled lonely most of the time. It hurts when you are the only one who doesn't get invited to a birthday party, or when someone calls you "towel head" or "camel jockey" instead of your real name. School can be a cruel place. Plenty of American kids got bullied after school, too, which brought the wimps together. But I was not allowed to enter even that fraternity. I won't lie: the isolation was often more than I could bear.

I hated being different. I remember wishing for a reverse tanning bed that would make me look whiter. I wanted so badly to blend in. I worked harder on having a Southern accent than building my vocabulary. Making sure my clothes matched was the last thing on my mind when I looked in the mirror. Instead, I would ask myself, *Do I look American enough today?* This is not a dilemma exclusive to immigrants. Everyone wants to fit in, wherever you're from. There is comfort in numbers, and maybe that's why things were so tough for the Nassers. Immigrants tend to form communities with each other in foreign lands. In the 1970s and '80s, for example, hundreds of thousands of Iranians flocked to Los Angeles, so much so that Los Angeles has been called "Iran-geles" and "Tehran-geles" by some. Had we moved to L.A., things might have been vastly different. But no. We chose a small military town in southern Texas. Not only were we the only Iranians we knew, we were the Iranians no one wanted to know.

Don't get me wrong. I share the blame for much of those lonely years. After a while, I just gave up trying to be accepted socially. It was easier to shut people out. After all, if I kept people at arm's length, they couldn't hurt me. I turned into a TV junkie who spent his afternoons feasting on a steady diet of mindless television. I guess the upside was that I learned to speak English more quickly than anyone else in my family. The Fonz, *The Brady Bunch*, and *Mork & Mindy* became my tutors after school and on the weekends. They taught me more than English. They shaped my sense of humor and my outlook on life in America. Shows like *Charlie's Angels* and *Wonder Woman* molded my idea of what a pretty girl looks like. *The Jeffersons*, *Sanford and Son*, and *What's Happening!!* educated me about the fact that immigrants were not the only ones on the receiving end of a little thing called racism. I speak English today without any trace of an accent, thanks in part to Hollywood.

My accent was not the only thing that went away. In applying for new birth certificates and a Social Security card, we had an opportunity to tweak our names, and took it. My sister and I took English first names. "Nastaran" became "Nancy," though she later went back to Nastaran to honor her roots. For me, Davood became David.

All this time, fifty-two Americans continued to be held hostage in the U.S. embassy in Tehran. In April 1980, the U.S. military and the CIA launched Operation Eagle Claw to rescue the American hostages. President Carter wanted desperately to free them before the presidential election that fall. I promise you, nobody wanted the hostages home from Iran more than me. But the operation was a disastrous failure. Miscommunication, a low-altitude sandstorm called a *haboob*, a fuel-truck explosion, and other problems forced the president to abort the mission, which cost eight American lives. After that, the hostages were scattered to make a second rescue attempt impossible.

Three months later the shah died of cancer. We wore black to school that day, not so much because our king had died as much as it was because my father's heart was broken. Dad knew too well of Shah Reza Pahlavi's shortcomings, but the death of his king meant the death of a kingdom. And this was the kingdom to which my father had pledged his allegiance.

My parents did not linger in their mourning. The shah's death seemed to re-focus and re-direct my father. I guess he finally realized we weren't ever going back. Dad took accreditation courses and added his U.S. commercial pilot's license to his military credentials in an effort to land a job. The problem was that no one was willing to take a chance on an Iranian refugee. He was a great pilot with a lot of flight hours and experience, but the market was flooded with Vietnam veteran pilots looking for jobs as well. Rightfully so, they were first in line.

Dad sent out dozens of applications, but everybody told him he was "overqualified." I sometimes wonder what would have happened if the cover letter to his application read, "Hello. Yes, I am an Iranian. But I have never held any Americans hostage. There are no Americans tied up in the trunk of my car or in my basement. I have never burned an American flag, and I too hate the ayatollah. Just because we all look the same doesn't mean we're all terrorists. Thank you. P/S. I really need a job because my kids love Baskin Robbins and that place ain't cheap."

As it turned out, the cover letter wasn't necessary after all, because on Inauguration Day, 1981, the hostages were released. The swearing-in ceremony of President Ronald Regan shared the headline space with homecoming pictures of the hostages. After 444 days, the ordeal was finally over. As we'd all hoped, not long afterward my dad got a job as a flight instructor with an aviation company working at Fort Rucker in Alabama. At last we would have some security and predictability in our lives again, a steady income, and a real sense of belonging. We didn't mind relocating if it made all that possible. We packed up the U-Haul filled with our American dream and exchanged one kind of South for another.

Enterprise, Alabama, the neighboring town to Fort Rucker, was somewhat familiar to my parents, as Killeen had been. My father had taken flight instruction there as well, way back before the revolution. On the drive, he told us the history of this small community, which was going to be our new address.

Enterprise is the city that owes it all to a bug. In fact, in 1919, the citizens of Enterprise erected a monument to none other than the boll weevil. It was, and still is, the only monument to an agricultural pest in the world. The cotton-loving boll weevil is indigenous to Mexico, but appeared in Alabama in 1915. By 1918, farmers all over the South were losing whole cotton crops to the beetle. Businessman H. M. Sessions saw this as an opportunity to convert the area to peanut farming since the peanut plant is immune to the insect. In 1916, he convinced C. W. Baston, an indebted farmer, to back his venture. The first crop paid off their debts and was bought by farmers seeking to change to peanut farming. Cotton was grown again, but farmers learned to diversify their crops, a practice which brought new money to the area.

That's when Bon Fleming, a local businessman, came up with the idea to build the monument and helped to finance the total cost. It's a tribute to how something disastrous can be a catalyst for change. The monument was dedicated on December 11, 1919, right smack dab in the middle of Main Street.

So, a plague had become a blessing in disguise. It took me years to realize how fitting it was that of all the towns in America, God had taken us to a city with which we shared so much in common. We too had gone through something disastrous that had eventually become a catalyst for change. For us, the plague had devoured so much more than cotton. It had disintegrated the very fabric of our nation. But, much like Enterprise, the Nassers had no choice but to persevere.

Enterprise, more than Killeen, was the America that my father had fallen in love with before the revolution. Alabama was easier than Texas for several reasons. First of all, we were more Americanized by then, and our Persian-to-English dictionary didn't need to be pulled out nearly as much.

Also, with the Iranian hostage situation behind us, Iran was no longer the main story in the news. As the heat was wearing off, so was the persecution. Neighbors actually brought over a welcome basket of chocolate chip cookies.

My dad joined the Lions Club and the Rotary Club. Life was getting better day by day. Mind you, it wasn't a bowl of cherries. Dad lost his job as a pilot, for example, but without skipping a beat he opened up an arts and crafts shop, which he and my mother ran together. Our store, proudly called Stitch-n-Stuff, put food on the table for seven years. More importantly, it gave my father a place to wear a suit and hold his head high. This was important to a man who would rather make a modest living wearing a coat and tie than twice the income wearing what he called *lebassa ashghali* (meaning "trashy clothes"). Stitch-n-Stuff started as a needlepoint and cross-stitch retail store (hobbies of my mother), but it morphed into a place that also offered custom framing, oriental rugs, and photocopying for nine cents a sheet. Customers could even get their Lions Club fruitcake there. It was a one-stop extravaganza.

As far as school was concerned, I was still a nerd who got bullied, but at least the 7-Eleven jokes and turban comments had become far too familiar to cut very deep. Did they really think they were the first to point at my bike and say, "Ali Baba, why are you riding a bike? Is your flying carpet broken?" I'd heard that one and all the others so many times, the jokes had lost their sting. I even managed to find a few friends, fellow geeks who huddled together for the occasional *Dungeons & Dragons* tryst.

All in all, Enterprise was the best kind of town, and I have fond memories of living at 104 Ladd Street. Our home was less than a mile from Enterprise State Junior College, which was basically thirteenth grade, but with ashtrays!

The Junior College also had tennis courts, and I quickly fell in love with the sport. Tennis is not a big deal in a town where football rules, but to me it was accessible. For other sports you needed a team, but for tennis you just needed a board to hit a ball against, or even better, one willing opponent. I found that opponent one summer in a neighbor who moved in across the street from us. His name was Craig Cosper. Craig was way too cool to be friends with a guy like me, but since he was new and it was summer, his options were limited. He and I became joined at the hip, riding our bikes to the tennis courts and baking for hours under the blazing sun. When Craig and I needed cash to fund our tennis habit, we cut grass or did anything else we could to keep the Gatorade flowing and the tennis balls bouncing.

Sometimes our landscaping business lost us more money than it made. Once when we were cutting grass, we found out the homeowner needed his pool cleaned. The water in the pool was slimy and green with algae, and we didn't have any experience. But when asked if we could help, we said sure, we can handle that. By the time it was all said and done, we had added too many chemicals and damaged the pool lining beyond repair. We tried covering up our mistake by pouring twenty bottles of blue food coloring in the pool. Needless to say, that fiasco did nothing to help our tennis careers.

Yes, Enterprise was a wonderful place—the kind of town where kids like Craig and I could ride our bikes from one end to the other, and where everything got fried, from the okra to the funnel cakes. Most driving directions in Enterprise included the phrase "Now, once you see the Piggly Wiggly . . ." And everyone went to church.

Everyone, except our family.

First Baptist Church of Enterprise, Alabama, was located steps away from the boll weevil monument right on Main Street, and it seemed *all* the "important" people went to First Baptist. The rest piled into First Methodist and the other churches in town.

One summer day, I was helping Dad out at Stitch-n-Stuff when a handsome man in a dark gray suit came into the store to buy some fruitcake. That in itself was odd, since no one ever came in exclusively for fruitcake. It was just something we had by the register to raise money for the Lions Club charity. The man looked like a movie star to me, the kind who got paid to smile. As I rang him up at the cash register, he asked me if I had to work every day of the summer, or if I got any days off for fun. I explained that I could take off, since I was related to the owner. He laughed and said, "Good! Then why don't you be my guest and come to VBS next week? Free of charge." He explained that VBS was a kids' camp, where for five days straight, from nine to noon, you played games and got free Pixy Stix. "How can you get me in?" I asked. "Oh, don't worry. I'll get you on the list." He grabbed a sheet of paper from the copy machine and wrote down "Special guest of Dr. Montgomery." Then he smiled and said, "Just look for the big tent set up on Main Street Monday morning, and give them this sheet of paper."

In hindsight, I can't believe I never put two and two together. I didn't realize that VBS was short for Vacation Bible School. It also didn't occur to me that Dr. Montgomery wasn't a medical doctor. He was, in fact, a doctor of divinity and the senior pastor at First Baptist, but I didn't know that yet. I was just excited to be invited to something.

That Monday morning, I rode my bike down Main Street looking for a tent. And there it was, under the shadow of a big church steeple. That's when I realized this was a First Baptist thing. I could hear the sound of music and kids my age playing inside. A sweet older lady approached me and said, "Come on in, sweetie. What's your name?" Not saying a word, I reached in my pocket and handed her the paper from Dr. Montgomery. "Ohhh," she said, "we've been waiting for you!" and so I followed her in. I honestly don't remember much about those next few days, except that we had to sing songs I'd never heard before and listen to boring stories told with a flannel graph about Jesus—you know, the man who was nice enough to let us into his country. The best part was the snacks. It was long ago, but I still recall the kindness of that lady in charge. Her Southern accent was as sweet as molasses, and she made sure "the visitor" (that was me) got the biggest scoop of chocolate mint ice cream.

After that week, Dr. Montgomery became a regular at our store. He dropped in from time to time to have something photocopied, even though I suspected the church office had a copier. He also came by for more Lions Club fruitcake, which, of course, no one eats.

7

Geek to Chic

Your dad just kissed me, dude." Rusty Weaver wiped his cheek as he walked through the door. He made sure he said it loud enough for everyone at the party to hear. I was petrified. Here I was, throwing my first real birthday bash, and Khosrow Nasser had taken it upon himself to welcome every guest with a Middle Eastern greeting, complete with a moustachey kiss on both cheeks.

Dad was ruining what I hoped would be my first real party. It had taken so much effort to get the party going. First I had to send invitations to every sixth grader in my school. I figured most of my classmates were too cool to hang out with me, but if all my geeky friends and a handful of bored cool people showed up, it could be a new start. Mom baked a cake in the shape of the space shuttle—she thought it genius that NASA sounded so much like Nasser. I had spent two days hanging records on the wall to transform our garage into a party pad. I even made two mix tapes—one with fast, fun songs and the other with slow ballads, in the hope of a love connection. But now, thanks to my dad, my dream was turning into a nightmare.

Thankfully, Nastaran came to the rescue. Realizing what was happening, she grabbed Dad by the hand and pulled him into the kitchen for a much-needed cultural lesson. Our lives had turned into a sitcom, filled with moments just like this. From stinking up the neighborhood with the awful smell of *kalapacha* (an Iranian delicacy of boiled cow tongue) to teaching classmates curse words in Farsi in an effort to be cool, being Iranian in Alabama had become less about being persecuted and more about being cultural misfits. While the party was somewhat of a success (I actually had real people show up), it ultimately didn't usher me into the next level of social involvement like I had hoped it would.

Then came high school.

It was the last day of the summer, and I was sitting in my room crying. I loved the summer, because tennis filled my days. Tennis had become a great equalizer. On the court, I could beat the cooler kids. They might have gotten the best of me everywhere else, but the tennis court knew no ethnicity. Now summer was over, and I had to go back to school.

Dad must have heard me. He walked into my room and asked, "Why the tears?" At first, I hesitated to open up, but after a few minutes, I began to explain that I was sad about having to go back to school. It was bad enough to be the geeky kid in elementary and middle school, but now high school was about to start. His response was surprising. Instead of the "toughen up" speech I was expecting, he told me to get in the car. Thirty minutes later we arrived at our destination. I guess we had been in America long enough to know where to go when you've got a sad teenager. The mall.

That afternoon, I got what some might call an extreme makeover. I got new clothes, a new haircut, new shoes, cologne, and a brand new school bag. Money was no object that day. If I liked it, Dad said yes. He was acting from pity, I knew, and that was just fine with me! My dad was trying to help me get a leg up and find acceptance. In reality, however, this was no way to help a son face the fires of high school. His intention was to pour a cup of water on the flames of insecurity, but it was more like a gallon of gasoline. And the flames took over.

I entered Enterprise High School dressed like an extra on the set of *Miami Vice*. Picture a pink tank top, white linen coat, and gray slacks, finished off with the ever popular black Ray-Ban sunglasses. This was what everybody in Hollywood was wearing, but we were nowhere near tinsel town. I realize now that I looked like a pastel flamingo. I was the same insecure kid on the inside, completely made over on the outside.

Everyone gets new clothes for the first day of school. I wanted a whole new identity.

And it worked. With my new style came instant attention. Not the kind I was accustomed to, but the sweetest nectar of attention that could be offered to a teenage boy. By first period, girls started talking to me in class. Once the girls like you, the guys who like the girls start liking the guy who can help them get the girls. It's all very confusing, but the bottom line is this: once you're in, you're in.

We all know we're not supposed to judge others by outward appearances, but, as we all know, most do. High school is no different. In many ways it's worse. The beautiful and the rich get all the perks, while the rest wait around for the leftovers. In the next few weeks, I learned how to play my new role in order to win at the popularity game. The formula has always been the same: wear the right stuff, listen to the right music, drive the right car, ignore the right people, and, last but not least, indulge in destruction.

It was in those early high school days when someone offered me my first beer. I took it, knowing it would not be my last. Drinking was the cool thing to do, so I did it. With reckless abandon. By the time I graduated, I was drinking all the time. I even snuck a flask filled with vodka to school sometimes and hid it in my locker. Eventually, alcohol became a gateway that led to other destructive behavior as well.

It was also in those days that I acted cold to my old "uncool" friends. Association with them was not good for my image, so I treated them like they were beneath me. By my senior year, I had become the very person who used to make fun of me when I was in middle school.

I put my brain on the top shelf and said, "I'm not going to need you anymore. Everyone else can find my identity for me. I will do what the 'in' crowd wants." And here's the irony: my friends and I thought we were rebels—by conforming precisely to MTV's definition of cool. We weren't rebels, we were fakes.

I had given up on my convictions in order to reserve a seat at the popular table in the lunchroom. High school was the place where the jocks and the cheerleaders ruled. If you weren't one of them, you had to offer something of value to be allowed in. I was willing to offer whatever it took.

In 1987, my parents announced that everyone in our family except Nastaran was moving back to Texas. My sister was moving to Birmingham, Alabama, for college. A friend of my dad's suggested we move to Plano, Texas, a suburb of Dallas, so that he and my father could start a construction company together. Looking for something new and exciting, we sold Stitch-n-Stuff and left Enterprise after seven years. I had entered that little town as a boy who didn't know much about American culture, but when we left, I was an expert. My accent was gone, and with it my naïveté about the American way of life.

"The Big Apple of the South" was everything I hoped it would be. Our stay in Dallas, or as we called it, D-town, only lasted a year, but in that short time I was able to feed the culture vulture in me even more. In Enterprise, we blasted the

Beastie Boys in our car stereos, but in Dallas we went and saw them live, two nights in a row. Back in Alabama, the biggest weekly gathering was the high school football game, but in Dallas it was the Cowboys in a stadium that held more people than all the citizens of Enterprise combined. We had six tennis courts by my old house in Enterprise. Plano boasted at least a dozen tennis clubs within a twenty-mile radius.

The stakes were much higher in D-town as well. The drug dealer at my old high school sold pot, but at Plano High, acid and cocaine were the designer drugs of choice.

I hit the ground running. I quickly made friends with guys who drove their dads' Ferraris to go clubbing and lived in multimillion-dollar houses. Most of my friends were much wealthier than I was, so I had to get a job to help fund all the expensive partying we did. I became a waiter at a restaurant called Café de France. It was a French bistro, owned by an Iranian family. We didn't know them personally, but being from Iran helped me land the job. I saw it as the perfect situation. Tips were mostly cash, so no one could track what I truly made as a salary. This kind of financial unaccountability was the only way I never got caught spending large amounts of money on what I now call the "sex, drugs, and 'prep-n-roll'" lifestyle.

One day, a kitchen chef at Café de France offered to sell me a dime bag of Mexican red bud that I could resell at street value. Within two months, I had bought and sold a hundred more bags of the top quality pot. The job at the restaurant became a front for my secret operation. It was my way to keep my parents from wondering why I had so much cash all the time. I remember having to find ways to spend it. It was nothing for me to take a dozen friends out to dinner at the best steak house in town. My friends and I went to every concert, got suites at the finest hotels downtown where we did our drugging, and paid off bouncers to frequent the best clubs.

My parents were so busy trying to survive that they themselves were too distracted to know any of this. Dad would work from sunup to sundown at the construction company, and Mom had her hands full with my little brother Benjamin. I stayed out late and slept in on weekends, but they presumed it was due to late hours at Café de France. There was so much they didn't know. They must have been relieved that I was not crying alone in my bedroom. To them, I had friends, a job, and I was doing okay in school. I covered up my indiscretions well, and they had no reason to ask questions.

Oh, how things had changed. At least when I was a nobody, I was David Nasser the nobody. Now I had become a gutless wonder who learned to play the game. Blinded by my own narcissism, I had become the worst kind of hustler. The suburban, designer-clothes-wearing, safe-looking liar, who lied to himself more than anybody else. I thought I was living the life in Dallas, but, in fact, life in Dallas was killing me. The last thing I wanted to do was leave, but it was the very thing I needed. Today I am personally thankful for the 1987 downfall of the economy in Texas, because the sagging building industry unexpectedly brought my father's new company to its knees.

That's when Dad decided to go into the restaurant business, even though he had no experience whatsoever in the field. His inspiration was the Café de France in Plano. The question arose, where to open this new venture? Alabama, of course. Mom wanted to get back to Alabama in order to be closer to my sister. Enterprise was two hours from her college campus, but Alabama's largest city, Birmingham, was only thirty minutes away. So in the summer before my senior year of high school, we moved once again, back to Alabama.

The moving yo-yo from Texas to Alabama, back to Texas, back to Alabama, was wearing thin. Over time we would build a new life, and then the fire of circumstances would burn it all to the ground. By now we had moved so many times, I had learned not to form deep attachments. I walked as a senior into the Birmingham suburban city school of Vestavia Hills not knowing a single person. Most of the senior class had grown up together, and here I was, the new guy, from a city that was six times larger than Birmingham. All my life, I had entered a school with the disadvantage of where I had come from; now, for the first time, I was in the driver's seat. The shock and awe of the experiences of my junior year easily captivated my new classmates. The most interesting thing was that I was not the kid from Iran. I was the kid from Texas. Things that don't really matter, seem to matter more in high school. "He only wears Armani," I heard a girl say as I walked through the hall. "I saw him pull out a roll of hundred dollar bills. He must be rich." This was intoxicating. The rumors were more glamorous and glitzy than the truth, but I was in no hurry to correct them.

With so much energy and effort focused on fitting in, I didn't spend a lot of time worrying about schoolwork that senior year. Most of my friends were headed to college, but I was struggling just to get out of high school. Somehow I squeaked by with a 1.9 GPA and graduated on time. I had spent so much effort worshiping the idol of social acceptance. Now that idol was about to crumble down on top of me.

After the graduation ceremony, I just sat in my car with my graduation cap on my lap. I hung the graduation tassel on my rearview mirror and watched the cars leave the parking lot one by one. I couldn't drive away. I was scared to leave. *Where do I go from here?* Graduation was supposed to be a moment of accomplishment, but I wondered exactly what I had accomplished that was worthy of any celebration.

We had escaped a bloody revolution for this? Was this the American dream?

8

WHEN GRACE WENT OUT TO EAT

Dark chocolate—the darker the better—followed by three sticks of cinnamon gum. It was a recipe I'd perfected through years of experience. Nothing covered up the smell of pot and alcohol better, and it had become a regular Saturday night ritual, usually followed by a mad dash from the front door to my room to change my smoke-drenched clothes. But this time, instead of avoiding my father when I got home, I headed straight to my parents' bedroom door and knocked.

Earlier that evening, as my friend and I sat in his smoke-filled car, I was venting about how depressing the situation was. All my other friends had graduated and were gone, it was Saturday night, and I had nothing better to do than sit in the car smoking dope with him. Since graduating, I had been working at my dad's restaurant and for some reason, I had this Saturday night off.

As he handed me the joint for one final hit, he asked, "Why don't you come to church with me tomorrow?"

I looked at him through bleary, red-rimmed eyes, giving my tainted brain time to process the question. Finally the words stumbled out. "You go to church?" I had no idea that he had any hint of spirituality in him.

"Oh yeah, I love church," he answered. "My church is awesome."

Until that night, we had never talked about God, religion, church, or anything of that nature. Our conversations generally revolved around girls, school, girls, tennis, girls, music, and parties filled with girls.

I told him I didn't want to go, and he wondered why not.

"I hate religion," I said. "When I was a kid I saw it destroy my country."

As he explained how his church was a big social playground, filled with teenagers we had gone to school with, it dawned on me why he loved his church. He attended to worship his first love. The one he could never shut up about, and the one he obsessed over more than anything else. Girls.

By the time he had named the five prettiest girls in our school and told me how they attended his church, I too wanted to go and pay homage.

There was just one problem. Dad. Islam was part of his culture and family tradition, and I figured that the idea of his son becoming a church attendee would not sit well. He'd given up so much of his heritage to move to America. Islam was one thing he wasn't about to let go of.

And so, after our deodorizing ritual, my friend and I went to my house. I marched to my parents' bedroom door and knocked.

"Hmm? What is it?" my father called out, his thick accent cutting through the darkness. "Are you okay?" I opened the door and eased in, leaving my friend waiting in the hall.

"I'm sorry to wake you up," I said. "I know you're going to say no. Just say it loud enough so my friend out in the hall will hear it and leave me alone. He wants to know if I can go to church with him tomorrow."

"Which church?" came his voice out of the darkness.

I was shocked. Why was he asking about specifics? Was he actually considering it?

I looked down the hall at my friend and asked him the name of his church. "Shades Mountain Baptist," he called out.

For the longest second there was silence, but then came my father's verdict. "I know those people," Dad said. "They are good people. You go there. But *only* there!"

I couldn't believe it. What I didn't know was that earlier in the week, some leaders from a local church had seen Dad and me scrambling to keep up with customers in his restaurant during a busy lunch hour. Instead of complaining about the slow service, these ministers rolled up their sleeves and started waiting on tables. They had come back several times since to volunteer again, and found other ways to help support his business. Their kindness had tenderized my father's heart to the point where, wonder of wonders, he was willing to let his son visit a church. But not just any church. The church my friend had invited me to was the exact same church the volunteer helpers were from. Unbelievable.

I thanked him and walked out of the bedroom to give my waiting buddy the news, not sure whether this whole thing was a good idea or not. Sure, church was an okay social gig, but everything that had ever happened to me in the name of religion was bad. This church thing had all happened so fast, I felt sucker-punched from both sides: first, getting invited by the last person on earth I thought would go to church, then getting the go-ahead from Dad when I was sure he'd say no.

The next morning, I put on my chinos and drove a short four miles to my friend's church in the 'burbs. I had driven by it countless times, but never on a Sunday morning. It looked like a giant ant farm that had been stepped on. What had always been a quiet cluster of buildings was now buzzing with a frenzy of activity. Everyone was dressed up and cheery, as if they were posing for a Norman Rockwell painting entitled "White Family Goes to Church." Hundreds of cars were pulling into the parking lot, while others filed out. This was no little chapel with a white steeple. This was Six Flags over Jesus! I was intimidated. I walked in and asked someone where all the teenagers met. He said they were having a Sunday school rally in the gym. *You have a gym?*

I had no clue what he was talking about. Muslims don't have small gatherings before the main service. I'd never heard of "Sunday school." What kind of ridiculous thing was that? I went to school Monday, Tuesday, Wednesday, Thursday, and Friday. I finally get a weekend off, and now there's Sunday school? Couldn't they at least call it something else?

A few minutes later, I found the gym and walked in to the smell of coffee and donuts filling the air. The room was packed with people my age standing around talking. Instantly, I recognized dozens of them. Some were acquaintances I partied and hung out with. I saw a girl I used to date, holding a donut in one hand and a Bible in another. As surprised as I was to see them, they were even more surprised to see me. I could see their eyes asking, "What's *he* doing here?" I walked up to the friend who'd invited me and greeted him with our usual salutation, "How the %*#@ are you, bro?" I knew better than to speak that way in a church, but it slipped out of habit. That's how we always talked to each other. But when he answered, he didn't talk like that at all. Nor did anybody else in the crowd. They were all using clean language, talking and acting completely differently than I'd ever seen them do before. They were walking around saying, "Bless you, bless you," and nobody was sneezing. What was wrong with these people? They reminded me of the movies they show on airplanes. The sanitized, cleaned-up version of the original.

My chlorinated friends were kind of embarrassed to be standing next to the blatant heathen, and gradually drifted away to other groups. One of the leaders, who I learned later was a youth pastor, got up on a stage at one end of the room and told everybody to take a seat. I happened to be near the stage and grabbed a chair in the front row. As the crowd all settled in and the noise died down, I noticed a very weird thing. The whole place was packed, except for the first two rows. I was sitting down front completely alone, surrounded by empty chairs. In most places, the audience wants to be as close to the stage as possible. If whatever was about to happen was so good, why did people want to sit so far away from it? What had I gotten myself into? As I tried to decide whether to put myself through this ordeal or run for the exit, I noticed someone heading straight toward me. A very large, muscular jock who looked like a compact version of a sumo wrestler. His name was Larry Noh.

Larry and I had met about a year earlier. He didn't go to my high school, but everybody knew Larry. He was the star linebacker at a rival school who could clean your clock. A rough guy on the football field who had a reputation for being outspoken about his faith. As a matter of fact, a year earlier, he had come up to me and three or four friends at a party and introduced himself, then pointed to the beer bottle in my hand. "I just wanted to tell you that alcohol and all this other stuff you're trying to fill your life with is never going to satisfy you. God told me to stop here at this party, get out of the car, and tell you and your buddies you need Jesus in your life."

We all started laughing. I laughed louder than anybody. We told him to get out of our face. Larry shook his head, and after a few more attempts, got in his car and drove away. Now, twelve months later, here he was heading straight at me. The last time, it had been four against one; now it was going to be one against four hundred Sunday schoolers with a linebacker leading the way. He was about to get me back big time.

His eyes were locked in, and it was obvious I was his target. "You're David Nasser. I remember you," he said, standing over me. That's exactly what I was afraid of. The only time we had ever met, I was such a jerk. But something stopped me from getting up and walking out. As calmly as possible, I said I remembered him too.

"It's amazing that you're here. This is an answer to prayer. Can I sit beside you?"

What? "Sure," I blurted. *Just don't sit on me and you can do anything you like.* Months later, I learned what he meant when he said that my being there was an answer to prayer for him. Even though he didn't go to my school, Larry had picked up a copy of our yearbook and circled pictures of ten seniors he believed were influencing people against Christ. He knew my reputation and had been praying for me by name long before I ever stepped one foot into his church.

The rally was starting. The speaker up front told everybody to get out his or her Bible. I didn't have one and was looking around self-consciously when I felt something on my lap. Larry had opened his Bible to the right spot and put it in front of me. For the rest of the talk, the two of us—the most blatantly out-of-place kid in the room and probably the most blatantly outspoken Christian in the room—sat side-by-side together in a row all to ourselves. I didn't hear a thing the teacher said. All I could think was, *why is this guy I was so mean to being so nice to me?*

When Sunday school was over, Larry bounced up and looked at me. "David, I'm really glad you came to hear this message," he said. "But I've got to confess something to you. I didn't listen to one thing that teacher was saying. All I could think about was you being here."

The suspense was killing me. I asked him why he was being so nice to me. Didn't he remember that night at the party?

"I remember," he said, then went right on with no further comment. "But you've got to come back tonight. The reason for the youth rally this morning is that we've got a big four-day event for youth starting tonight. You've got to come back for it. It'll be awesome."

I had nothing on the calendar, but pride kept me from accepting his invitation. I remembered feeling pitied back in the fifth grade, when I had attended Vacation Bible School. It wasn't anything the kind old lady who taught VBS had done, but rather the strange feeling I had that these people thought they were better than me or that they had something

I didn't have. Whatever it was, I didn't like it, and I didn't want to feel that way again. So I lied and told Larry I had something else to do.

"Okay. If you won't come to our house, we'll come to yours," he replied with a gleam in his eyes.

I didn't know what that meant. "Whatever. Thanks for letting me use your book," I said, handing him back the Bible.

The next night, at about six o'clock, I heard a knock at our door. When I opened it, I saw a handful of teenagers standing on the front porch with Larry Noh front and center.

"Hey man, I told you if you couldn't come to our house, we'd come to yours. Can we come in for a few minutes?" Larry grinned.

I was too surprised to say no. "What is this?"

"It's called visitation. We go and see people who've come to our church. We just hang out and visit with you."

I stepped aside and they came trooping in. I actually knew one of them better than Larry. His name was Marshall. Marshall would occasionally hang with my clique of friends in high school. He partied with us, and seemed as girl crazy as I was, but never got involved in drugs or alcohol. We loved him because he could always be our designated driver. I always thought he just had strong morals, but now he was walking into my house with a Bible. *Uh-oh, they're going to try to convert me.* They sat down, and my mother, glad to meet such a polite group, offered them a drink. We sat and talked about the weather, and about anything else we could think of, except the one thing I knew they were there to expound on. Then Larry spoke up.

"David, we came over here tonight because you are very valuable to us. We care about you so much that we wanted to tell you about the most important decision anyone could ever make in life."

Here comes the pitch.

"David, what do you know about Jesus Christ?" Larry asked.

"I know that you are Christians, and that he is your religious leader. Look, I don't have a problem with him. After all, he helped us get to America," I said jokingly.

"What do you mean?"

I smiled and said, "Nevermind."

Larry didn't miss a beat. "He is more than a leader," Larry said. "He is the Son of God. But most importantly, he loves you so much, David, that he paid the penalty for your sins, by dying on a cross for you. Three days after his death, he proved that he was God by coming back to life. His death, burial, and resurrection are the only hope you have to find forgiveness from your sin. David, you're a sinner in need of a savior, and Christ wants to save you from hell."

He had lost me a few words back, so I asked questions. Larry and the rest of the gang answered the best they knew how. Their answers were sprinkled with religious language that I had a hard time understanding, but I could see that they wholeheartedly believed what they were saying. Over and over again, they kept referring to the Bible as if it was the answer book to all my questions.

Somewhere in the conversation Marshall piped in, "God loves you, David, and you don't have to clean yourself up to come to God. He loves you just the way that you are. He always has. He wants to give your life meaning and purpose."

That was a revolutionary thought. Jesus loving me just the way I was? Jesus wanting me to have a good life? Sure he loved people like Larry Noh—he was a good guy who did saintly deeds—but I was different. I was a self-obsessed little prep who didn't want to have anything to do with God.

"Are you sure he loves me? Are you sure he wants me to have a great life? Because my life has been pretty tough so far, and I think some of it is God punishing me for all the bad stuff I've done."

"He doesn't love you because of what you've done or what you haven't done. He loves you because he's a loving God. He loves you no matter what you've done."

That was the first time I'd ever heard about any connection between religion and unconditional love. God loved me despite my behavior? All my life, I'd been taught I had to do things to get God to love me. Religion was based on rules: the better you followed them, the better person and the closer to God you were. I had to earn God's love, follow the rules, toe the line—or else. And now these Christians were telling me God loved me regardless. They called it grace. God's unmerited love for me, a gift I couldn't earn, no matter what I did or didn't do.

It sounded too good to be true, so I wasn't buying it. "Nah, thanks for coming over. I'm not interested." Part of it was my pride talking. But I was also worried that if I believed them and became religious, there would be a bait-and-switch act coming. I thought that *if I believe, the catch is that I'll have to stop doing a lot of the things I liked.* These Christians seemed like they had nothing better to do on Sunday than go to Sunday school. On Saturday they probably had Saturday school. And on Monday, here they were coming over witnessing to people. I wanted no part of this cult or clan or whatever it was.

As they were leaving my house, Larry said nonchalantly, "We'll see you next week."

"Yeah, sure, whatever."

By the time they left, I had more questions than answers, but I had a hunch that they were not afraid to try and answer every one of them. The next Monday, they were back at my house again, and the next Monday, and the next. As six o'clock on Monday evenings approached, I would think, *Hide! The Christians are coming!* We had become the Iranians who were being terrorized by a bunch of zealots.

Every Monday, I answered a knock at the door, and there were Larry and a few others. As much as I wanted not to like them, I noticed one very special thing that never changed from week to week: they focused less on how bad I'd been, and more on how great Jesus was. They didn't criticize my culture or say anything bad about Islam. Every conversation seemed to revolve around Jesus. It was always about him.

They didn't seem interested in getting me to stop drinking or cursing or watching certain movies. They weren't interested in my behavior or any kind of checklist. They kept talking about the greatness of Jesus, instead of the badness of David Nasser. They never talked about what great Christians they were. Larry never sat me down and told me all the things he was doing right in his life because of Jesus. He just kept teaching me about Jesus. Everything came back to Jesus.

The Monday visits were only part of the circus. Just about every Wednesday and Sunday, at least one guy would show up at my house in time to drag me to church. I say they dragged me, and that's what my pride would have made me tell anybody. But if they were ten minutes late, I'd peek out from behind the curtain, wondering where they were. I expected them, and deep down I wanted them to come far more than I realized. Not that I wanted to learn about their religion, I just wanted to be with them. Religion is not a magnet, but love is. These people loved me unconditionally, and I wanted to be with them because I craved their love. I knew boyfriend/girlfriend love, I knew mom and dad love, and I knew brother/sister love. I'd heard all kinds of "I love you's" in my life. But I had never heard that people could love you despite how you had treated them.

After church, I'd go hang out with some of the students who visited me at home. Sometimes Marshall would come over at random times just to hang. Occasionally I would push the boundaries to see how he would react. Cursing, bragging, mocking—whatever I did, he answered with kindness. I would tell a dirty joke, and most of the time he would not laugh. I say most, because once in a while he would crack a smile. I was actually glad to see him struggle with holding back laughter at my questionable humor. It meant he was human. Once I saw him lie to his girlfriend about why he was late for dinner. Later on, he confessed he was lying, and asked for forgiveness. It made me realize that Christians were regular people who messed up as well. That little incident actually drew me closer to them, because all of a sudden they didn't seem so perfect. It made me realize that they needed the same grace that they were extending to me. Marshall and I even got jobs at my dad's restaurant so we could hang out more. We would talk for hours about life and matters of faith. He didn't have all the answers, but he was there to listen.

Larry, Marshall, and the rest had a genuine faith that baffled me. All my life, I'd associated God with rules and retribution. But they attributed the possibility of a relationship with God to this thing called grace. They would explain for the millionth time: "We're not great. This is God's unmerited love flowing out of our lives." For the longest time, I didn't get it. But then I saw it firsthand, and that changed everything.

A few weeks before Christmas, seven of us jammed ourselves into Larry's Honda after Sunday night church and went out to eat. It was late, none of us were really that hungry, and we were a bunch of teenagers being louder than we needed to be in a restaurant. Our waitress was not happy. She rolled her eyes, took our order with a grumpy attitude, and gave us service that was mediocre at best. She was tired and in no mood to deal with a bunch of high-maintenance, dessert-only kids. We finished and left. As they always did, somebody paid for my food. These nights out never cost me a dime.

When we piled back into Larry's car, I ended up sitting on two people, scrunched against the back seat window on the driver's side. As Larry started backing out of the parking space, I heard a loud *tap tap tap* an inch from my left ear. I turned toward the sound and saw our waitress right in my face at the window, our noses separated only by the thickness of the glass. Larry slammed on the brakes, rolled down my window, and then craned his neck around to look at the waitress. Because of the car next to us, she couldn't get to his front door to talk to him, so she poked her head through my window, as Larry twisted around to face her. Now our three noses were almost touching.

"Get out of the car!" she yelled. If only she'd been that energetic when she was waiting on us.

"Get out of the car!" she repeated, short of breath from her run outside.

"What is it?" Larry asked.

She said she'd just been chewed out by her boss for not stopping us. We'd made a big mistake and overpaid. By a lot. The bill was thirty dollars, and we left more than one hundred and thirty. She held up a wad of bills.

Larry smiled. "Ma'am, that wasn't a mistake. We know it's nearly Christmas, and we know you're working hard. We got you at the end of a long and tiring day. We just wanted to bless you, so we emptied out our pockets. If we'd had more, we'd have given you more. And we'll be back next week."

The waitress yelled right in my ear. "Make sure you get my table!" Big tears welled up in her eyes and came down her face. I looked at Larry, that massive hulk of a linebacker, and he was crying too. Everybody in the car was crying. *I was crying!* I couldn't help it. We left her in the parking lot clutching the tip of a lifetime. Watching her as we pulled away, I thought to myself, *so that's grace. Grace is getting the very opposite of what you deserve.*

The first time he came to my house, Larry said, "Jesus doesn't love you because you're good. He loves you because *he's* good." All that stuff I'd been hearing in church hour after hour, singing songs about amazing grace, stumbling through the Bible verses—it all made sense, all came to life in that moment, in the back seat of an overloaded Honda in a restaurant parking lot. In that instant, the light went on. I had a hard shell around me to keep religion out. Religion had destroyed my security, threatened my life, and turned my family into refugees. I wanted nothing to do with religion.

Now I realized my Christian friends didn't want religion either. They wanted Jesus Christ. The shell that had kept religion out of my life had also kept Christ out. But that night it cracked.

9

WATER WALKER

They say tears are the way home.

After that tear-filled night in the Shoney's parking lot, I became less cynical and jaded about the things of God. What initially drew me to my new Christian friends was the kindness they showed me, but now I was intrigued by something bigger. They cared for me, but nowhere near as strongly as they cared about loving and serving their God. The funny thing was I wasn't threatened by this; in fact, their love for God over me became my favorite thing about them. For me, it was the best kind of demotion. The kind you welcome when you find yourself wanting less attention, so that people can give their attention to one who deserves it.

I had spent so much of my adolescence as a self-worshipper; now, I wanted off the throne. Don't get me wrong. I was not ready to let Jesus take over as king, but I knew I was not fit to rule my own life.

Like my homeland, I had become a kingdom without a king.

One frigid Sunday night, I went to church—by myself this time. No one had to pick me up. I knew I wanted to go, and so I called Larry and told him that I would meet him in the sanctuary. It seemed so silly to act like I didn't need help anymore. I was tired of playing games. It had been several weeks since grace dropped in on a tired waitress, and I was forever changed. Something real was happening to me.

I sat with Marshall as we listened to the pastor preach. Dr. Charles T. Carter was an "Old Rugged Cross" kind of preacher. In just about every sermon, he would hold his hand up to his ear and lean in to let everyone know he was waiting for an "Amen!" He was a Southern gentleman who, judging from his sermon illustrations, had deep affection for quail hunting and fresh Waffle House coffee. He was kind. Meek out of the pulpit, but a fireball in it. That night was no exception. Dr. Carter preached about heaven, and he preached about hell. A hell we all deserved, and a heaven that awaited those who had been forgiven of their sins. Then came the invitation, filled with fervent appeals of, "Come on down!" and "Step out of your seats!"

I remember thinking, if the gospel is such good news, why is he so mad? But deep down I knew he was not mad, just passionate. He loved us enough to tell the truth. Even if it was the last thing some wanted to hear. During the invitation, strange feelings roiled inside me. For one thing, I was scared. I knew I deserved the very hell Dr. Carter preached about.

Every time Larry, Marshall, and the others had talked about Jesus, the light of his greatness revealed to me the sins of my yesterdays. And I knew if unforgiven sin meant death, I had much to fear. What shocked me more than anything was Dr. Carter's confession that he deserved hell too. I knew that a bad person like myself deserved such a horrific destination, but he was not pointing fingers at me and my behavior. He was pointing a finger at all of humanity and our souls. At that moment, I began to understand that my outward behavior was merely a symptom of who I was deep down inside. A sinner who stood guilty before a sinless God. This reality was both sobering and scary, to say the least.

So I stepped out of the pew and into the aisle. As others were going forward, I turned around and walked straight to the back door. I wanted to get out of there as soon as I possibly could.

Earlier in my life, I'd been terrorized by religion, and now it felt like this guy was trying to scare me down an aisle. But I knew this: what I felt was not the fear of tyrannical authorities, it was the conviction of truth.

I got in my car and slammed the door. These people were starting to get to me. These strange feelings were coming at me too fast. I decided I wasn't coming to this or any church ever again. Things were getting out of hand, and it was time for me to take charge of the situation.

The house was empty when I pulled in that night. My parents and brother were in Atlanta, and my sister was away at college. Good. They wouldn't be around asking me to explain why I seemed so rattled. As I walked into my bedroom, I saw on the corner of my dresser the stack of Bibles that had been given to me by different people in the youth group. In the last few months I'd been given several Bibles, heard all about the Bible, listened to people read the Bible, and even made a few comments about the Bible, but I had never cracked one open myself.

Like a wounded animal that bites a helping hand, I walked over to the stack of Bibles and grabbed one while sliding open the patio door that led out of my room. I walked over to the barbeque grill and dropped it in. While dousing the book with charcoal fluid, I realized how this over-the-top symbolic gesture was not going to take away any of these feelings, but I didn't care. I was angry. If Dr. Carter was going to preach about fire and damnation to scare me, I was going to start a few flames myself.

I was angry at a God who let so much pain and loneliness come to my family and me. A God who now, after all these years, dared to ask for my heart. In that moment, I was smart enough to know there was a God, but dumb enough to confuse him with bad religion. I wanted to set a Bible and everything and everyone it represented on fire, so that I could watch it all burn before my eyes. But I could not find a single match.

In times like this, all you can do is laugh. I looked everywhere. In the kitchen, in the nightstand, behind the grill, but the more I looked, the more it became obvious how I couldn't even blaspheme God without being an unprepared fool.

What now?

Was God asking his angels to hide the matches because there was an Iranian on the loose? Was he a cosmic prankster? Or could it have been the wisdom of a loving father, who sets the matchbox on the top shelf to keep a child from harming himself?

Okay, okay, you win. I'll open it.

I could have gone back in and grabbed a dry Bible, but why stop the insanity now? I grabbed the fluid-soaked book and started from the beginning. Literally. The Bible starts with those exact words: "In the beginning . . ."

The sentences were long and convoluted. The text was full of strange words and expressions, and the stories took forever to get through. It was one of the most boring books I'd ever read in my life. I couldn't believe those guys brought me all these copies of the same book. I couldn't understand how hundreds of millions of people based their lives on its teaching. The only parts that weren't boring were the parts where I was too confused to be bored. But for some reason, I kept flipping through it—its pages soggy, smelly, and stained with greasy charcoal fluid.

That's when I came to a story in the book of Matthew. The story was about a man named Peter who, one night while in a boat with some friends, sees Jesus walking toward him on top of the water. What made the story so intriguing was not the fact that Jesus is walking on the water (after all, he is supposed to be God), but that Peter asks Jesus if he too can step out and be a water walker. I expected Jesus to say something like "I can perform miracles, but you're not me. Stay in the boat." But instead, he simply says, "Come." Then the story gets better. Peter gets out of the boat and starts walking. All of a sudden you have a guy who is God and another who has faith in God, and they are walking on water toward one another. It hit me like a flash of lightning.

That's what I'm supposed to do.

Jesus was calling me to step out of the boat. *This is crazy,* I thought. But I had stepped out of the boat for so many other things in my life. I'd stepped out for social acceptance, for family, for friends—but they had all left me sinking. The only one who could give me the real power to walk was the one I'd never completely trusted. Through the pages of a smelly Bible, Christ was asking me to trust him—right there, right then.

The same Bible that had bored me five minutes earlier came alive. It wasn't some old-time story. Jesus was alive in the Bible I was about to burn, speaking to me through the Word of God, saying, "Trust me."

I walked back into my bedroom and sat on my bed. Even though I was the only one in the house that night, for the first time ever I did not feel alone. I sat there for a while, trying to figure out what to say. Finally, I lifted my head and my hands, and I whispered, "Save me."

"Save me from my sins, from my excuses, from bad religion. From my own agenda. From trying to live life on my own terms. Save me from all of it. Save me from myself."

10

STORMY WATERS

I didn't hear them come in. The sound startled me.

"What's wrong?" Mom asked.

I looked up to see my parents standing in my bedroom. They had arrived from their trip to Atlanta to find their son lying on his bed, weeping. It was well past midnight, and I should have been asleep, but who could sleep on such a night?

All I could say over and over was, "I love him! I love him! I love him!"

"You love who?"

"Jesus! I love Jesus!"

Dad maintained his composure, and after a moment of silence said, "Go to bed. It's late. We'll talk to you in the morning." And that was that. Without another word, they left me and went to the other room.

Judging from my past, they probably weren't all that worried. I had started and stopped a lot of things. I started playing the guitar; now it was collecting dust in a corner. I took up surfing for a while, even though the nearest ocean was four hours away; my surfboard hadn't touched water in years. And there were the tennis lessons that never turned into a career. I assume they were thinking that now I had a Bible and loved Jesus, but I would eventually get over that too. It was just a stage I was going through.

With all the excitement, it was impossible to sleep. At 2:30 in the morning, I thought about the youth pastor of the church I'd been attending. Allen had given me his phone number and said if I ever wanted to talk or ask a question, I could call him day or night. I had to call somebody, and I knew that most of my friends would get in trouble if I called so late. So I called the only adult Christian whose number I knew.

After a few rings came a very sleepy "Hello?"

"Hey, this is David Nasser. Remember me?"

"Yeah, man. It's the middle of the night, are you okay?"

"Yeah. Listen, I asked Jesus to save me tonight."

"All right! I'm so glad!" He was gracious enough to talk with me for a while, and then he said a prayer before we hung up.

The next morning I called Larry and Marshall. You would have thought they won the lottery. I think they were more excited than I was. By afternoon, news had spread throughout the entire youth group about my conversion, and they threw a birthday party for me to celebrate my spiritual rebirth. There we were at Shoney's, once again, basking in the grace of God. It felt like I had found the cure for a disease, and I wanted to share the remedy. When it was time to leave and go to Monday night visitation, I went with them, eager to tell others about my new identity. Everything was going so well, it felt like I was skipping on the waves with Jesus.

But a storm was gathering.

Someone from the church contacted me about scheduling a baptism, explaining that baptism is a public profession of what Jesus had done in me personally. I wanted to get baptized, but I knew Mom and Dad would not approve.

Dad had started to get a little nervous already. Although Dad and I never officially talked about my conversion, his silence sent a very loud and clear message. Maybe this wasn't going to be like the guitar after all. It was more his pride than anything to do with Islam. He'd lost his position in the army, his fortune in Iran, his social pedigree, and now, thanks to his wayward son, he was losing his religious heritage.

In my father's mind, I had become the prodigal, the one who was trying to lead the family astray with all this Jesus talk.

I did not need his permission to get baptized, so I decided not to tell them about it until one hour beforehand.

"Where are you going? Why do you have a gym bag with you?" my mom asked.

"I'm going to get baptized tonight. I'm taking a change of clothes and some hair stuff since I'll be getting wet in the baptism pool."

Dad overheard and walked in to speak to me.

"That's it," he said, "we've had enough."

He explained how for the past few weeks they had patiently let me go through this phase, and now it was starting to become a nuisance. In Birmingham, my parents had found a small group of Iranians to befriend. Most of these Iranians were doctors, scientists, professors, and other well-educated professionals like my parents. They were as devout as Mom and Dad when it came to Islam, but my father knew if word got out about my becoming a Christian, there would be gossip and embarrassment.

This small community served an important purpose in our lives, because it was a place for us to connect with people of the same nationality. We celebrated Iranian holidays together and enjoyed their company.

"You're not a Christian," he explained. "We're a Muslim family."

We were? The most devout I ever saw my father was at that moment. My mother had taught me Arabic prayers called *sala*, but we didn't face Mecca even once a day, much less the five times we were required by the pillars of Islam. Growing up, I was told a few stories about Muhammad, but we never read the Qu'ran together. We had never visited a mosque in

America (there are over a thousand), and for us, fasting at Ramadan was sporadic at best.

Now we were Muslims?

Dad's eyes drilled into me. His patience was exhausted. "That's it," he ordered. "You will stop being a Christian."

How do I stop being a Christian?

That's like holding up a piece of plywood to stop the Niagara Falls. The grace I had received was far too powerful to be stopped.

I let my father know in no uncertain terms that I was going to be baptized. This was a first for me. I had disobeyed my father plenty of times, but never to his face. We stood there face-to-face for a moment, and then I turned and walked toward the front door.

"I'm going to be late. I'm getting baptized tonight."

To some, that might seem like a great moment of exercising my faith; but in time, I've learned that I was exercising my rights more than anything else. I was so immature in my relationship with Christ that I never took the time to really think it through. What if I had stayed home that night? Not stopped being a Christian, but just waited to get baptized until a later time? Being baptized was a great thing, but I shouldn't have used it to defy my parents. I could have gone about it in a different, more loving way.

What was I thinking, that Mom and Dad would say, "We never knew Jesus loved us and had a wonderful plan for our lives until our son blatantly disobeyed us. Thank you, David!" I wish I had been smarter about it.

Others were being baptized that night as well. I specifically remember a little girl who went into the baptism pool before me. She must have been nine or ten. From where I stood, I could see her parents, friends, and relatives sitting in the audience. They were there to enjoy the special moment with her. I wished so much that my parents could have been there, too. I wanted to say, "I want to wait, I've changed my mind, I can't do this just yet," but I was afraid to disappoint my friends and my new church. They had done so much for me. Besides, I already had the white robe on and everything. So when my turn came, I stepped down into the warm water of the baptistry, not realizing that a baptism by fire was waiting for me at home.

When I got back to the house, Mom and Dad were sitting in the living room, waiting.

"Give me your house key," he said. As I reached in my pocket, Iranian curse words came gushing out of him, as if all this emotion had been brewing while I was gone. My entry had broken the dam, and it was all pouring out now.

His son had disobeyed a direct order. To him, this was as if I had spit in his face. I had dishonored him, and what's worse, I had done it in front of my mother.

We might have been living in Alabama, but strict Iranian protocol was still the law of our home. For example, I never walked through a doorway in front of my parents, but rather followed a few steps behind them. I was taught to take only the smallest piece of chicken from the serving tray, to honor the elders with the larger portions. I always stood up and spoke greetings when someone entered a room, and no matter how tired I was, I never slouched or reclined when I was with people older than me. I excelled in the delicate balancing act of *taarof*, an interesting and elaborate system of deference and politeness. Above all, you never, ever explicitly and publicly disobey parental direction. All of this was the expected behavior of good Iranian boys. We Iranians are a complex people, and through my blatant lack of submission I had brought my father shame.

"You are dead to me," he went on, solemnly. "You are no longer my son. Go."

Mother quickly interjected. "We're not kicking out our own son."

Hell hath no fury like a mother's defense! No one was letting her baby boy spend the night as a homeless man. She wasn't approving my decision to follow Christ, but she was still my mom, and she let my father know it.

I wept as I watched them fight. I thought about the little girl who had been baptized with me. I wondered if her family had gone out to eat afterward, and how many rolls of film they emptied, snapping pictures of their daughter's proud moment.

I knew then it was time to leave. Maybe not at that moment. But soon, very soon. Mom begged me to stay, but I knew life would be difficult for her, most of all, if I stayed.

Maybe Marshall or Larry would let me stay with them.

As early in my walk with God as it was, I learned that being a Christian doesn't mean life gets easy. Getting out of the storm-tossed boat does not guarantee life will be easy sailing later on.

Just a few weeks before, I read the story of a man named Peter who stepped out of a boat to walk toward Jesus. God used that story to speak to me. "Have faith, deny yourself, trust me, and come" were the words I had heard, but I knew there was more to the story. Both for Peter and for me.

When Peter first steps out on the water, he is calm. The first few steps must have been exhilarating. But soon a storm blows in, and Peter feels the waves begin to churn beneath his feet. The calm waters become a raging sea. Peter, not surprisingly, is terrified. He takes his eyes off Jesus and looks at the storm. That's when he begins to sink.

It dawned on me after my parents' fight that I was in my first storm as a Christian. It was raging all around me, demanding my attention.

The good news in Peter's story is that though he was sinking, at least he knew whose name to cry out.

"Jesus!"

Why didn't he yell to the guys behind him in the boat? "Hey, I'm drowning over here, hand me a paddle?" Why didn't he curse the one who had asked him to step out in the first place? "I can't believe you got me in this mess, Jesus!"

Why? Because Peter knew the safest place in the storm was not the boat, but as near as he could be to Jesus.

Jesus comes to Peter's rescue, not with an "I told you so" sermon, not after Peter drank a few sips of saltwater to learn his lesson. No, Jesus came immediately.

The Bible says Jesus pulls Peter up and brings him back into the boat. By the end of the story, we see an image that is both beautiful and haunting. The storm has died down, and both men are in the boat. Peter is soaking wet; Jesus is completely dry, except for the bottoms of his feet. And Jesus embraces Peter.

Jesus then looks at Peter and whispers, "You of little faith, why did you doubt?"

In the stormy waters of those next few days following the fight and my decision to move out, all I wanted to do was keep my eyes on Jesus.

As I closed the door and walked away from my parents' home, I had a distinct sense that Jesus was holding me.

11

THE RIGHT KIND OF FEAR

The Solid Rock Café. Think Hard Rock, but "Christianized."

When my youth pastor, Allen, made the announcement that he was leaving our church to fully devote his time to opening and managing a Christian nightclub, everyone in our youth group was ecstatic. We weren't losing Allen, we were gaining a place to hang out. No more Shoney's. The purpose of the Solid Rock Café was to give the teens in our area a positive environment to hang out in, so they could stay out of trouble. An out-of-business fitness facility had been transformed by filling the pool with cement and restructuring a few walls. There was a game room on one side and a concert hall on the other. The mirrors from the gym stayed, so the concert hall appeared twice as big. It even had a café, where you could get food named after biblical characters, such as the Samson Hoagie, the Jonah Fish Sandwich, and the Doubting Thomas Donut. The food was actually pretty good, as long as you stayed away from the Armageddon Special—a chili dog with hot sauce and onions.

The club couldn't have come at a better time. Allen needed interns to work the club, and he was offering to hire me, Larry, Marshall, and a few other guys from our youth group. Our salary was free rent. We still had to pay the cable and the electricity, but the actual rent was paid for by the club. In a time when I really needed a place to stay, this was an answer to prayer.

The guys and I lived in a small, older apartment complex. The kind you see on the six o'clock news. I had left the comforts of a nice house with a mother who did my laundry for me and a fridge filled with good food for a bachelor pad that had more roaches in the cabinets than dishes. How life had changed. I went from rich and unfulfilled to broke and satisfied. I remember eating ramen noodles for weeks on end because I didn't have enough money to eat at the Solid Rock most of the time. Allen offered us half-off anything we wanted as an employee discount, but I needed every penny for gas and every quarter for the laundromat. Someone must have told Allen, because he put me in charge of the kitchen.

"I need you to sample the food every day as a measure of quality control. I'm moving the other interns from the café and putting you in charge of it, since you have experience in the restaurant business with your dad's place and all." He was "making" me eat on his dime. Sure, Larry had the cool job of hosting the events in the concert hall, and Marshall got a key to the video game machines in the arcade, but I got free food.

Little by little, God was supplying my every need. I remember the first month when my share of the cable and electricity bill was due. It was eighty-three dollars. I avoided my roommates like immigration. I knew they were broke too, and they would not be able to pay the bill until I coughed up my portion. Once again, Allen came through.

"Can you go and fill in for me at an evangelistic event next Sunday night? I was supposed to be the guest speaker, but I have to back out. They'd love to hear the story of how you came to know Christ." He explained it was a small country church; twenty-five people or so would attend. I was thrilled to get to speak, so that Sunday I put on my suit and went to serve.

The service went great—so great in fact that in all the excitement, they forgot to take the love offering they intended to give to their guest speaker. I remember walking out of the church and thinking how glad I was that God had moved so powerfully, but I also remember wishing he had moved powerfully in a financial way as well. I didn't have money to fill the tank in my car, much less the eighty-three dollars I owed my roommates.

Just as I was about to leave, the pastor yelled out my name.

He approached me and let me know how thankful he and his congregation were that I had come. As we stood by my car and talked about the night, out of nowhere he got a look of shock on his face. "Oh no! We forgot to take the offering!" I told him not to worry about it.

The pastor turned around and saw the only other two men in the church parking lot. They were church leaders who had stayed behind to turn off the lights and lock the front door of the small sanctuary.

"Wait here for just a second," he told me.

The pastor jogged over to them, and after a minute I saw all three men walking toward me. "Son, we're sorry we forgot your offering." Then all three men reached into their back pockets and got out their wallets. They unfolded them and emptied every bill out into the pastor's hands. This man of God counted the money and looked up with embarrassment. "So sorry, Brother David, all we have tonight is eighty-three dollars. Will that do?"

I could tell you story after story like that. Moments when God would allow me to come to that "How am I going to make it?" crossroads, only to work a miracle to increase my faith in him.

Through the eyes of faith, the world seemed new and exciting and full of potential. I was a clean slate, and I wanted to know everything about Christ and Christianity. I couldn't learn it fast enough, couldn't wait to make up for lost time. When not working at the club, I filled my days with study. The guys I lived with went to college, but since I didn't have the money, I decided to educate myself with Christian studies. I went to the church library and got as many books and videos as I could find. One of the best resources for filling the gaps in my Bible knowledge that first year turned out to be kids' Christian videos. I watched the animated Bible stories because most of the adult resources were a little over my head.

I tried to read my Bible for at least an hour a day, sometimes staying up late to finish a chapter, only to get dragged into another, and another. It didn't matter, I loved it. I strained to understand the context, plowing away, reading and absorbing everything I could get my hands on. I just couldn't wait to make up for lost time.

No matter how much of Jesus I packed my days with, sometimes at night I would lay there in bed, staring at the ceiling. Often lustful and impure thoughts would roam through my mind. The sins of my past had been forgiven, but not forgotten. Finally, one night, I'd had enough. The next day, I headed out to the church library with a game plan. "I'm going to tape a big poster of Jesus on my ceiling," I thought to myself, "so that I can stare at him at night. If he is watching over me, the bad thoughts won't dare come back." Three hours later, I found myself frustrated because I couldn't find a single stern, harsh-looking picture of Jesus. These smiling Jesuses just weren't going to cut it. I needed a picture of Christ looking somewhat disappointed at my inner thoughts.

After a long search, I finally found one. It was a very angry looking Jesus turning over the money changers' tables in the temple. I had it enlarged on a photocopy machine in the biggest size available. I then cut out just his face and torso. I took it home and taped it to the ceiling directly over my bed, so that when I looked up, the fiery eyes of "angry Jesus" could serve as my lust repellant. There he was, my overhead accountability.

Those were the days of radicalism. I didn't have much depth, so I tried to overcompensate with effort. I wanted so badly for my life to count for Christ. But at that moment, no one was really teaching me how to run a spiritual marathon instead of a 100-yard dash. I had the pedal to the metal.

For example, a few of the people in the youth group would get in the car on a Saturday night and someone would ask what everybody wanted to do. One would suggest a movie, another wanted bowling. Someone else might have voted for just having a laidback dinner. But I always said the same thing, "Let's go find some people and tell them about Jesus." After that, any other suggestion sounds like a selfish, pagan thing to do. After all, there were lost people going to hell, and we needed to go tell them how they could be saved!

Nothing is more annoying than a brand-new Christian with a bad case of the "I-just-got-saved-ies." I must have driven a lot of people crazy in those days. I just wish they had spoken up. The ones who were brash about their own faith were not the ones I annoyed. No, they were the Christians who saw these kind of instances in my life as a sign that I was ready to lead.

Honestly, what I needed was a chill out, but instead it seemed that I was placed on a spiritual pedestal. I was way too young in my faith to have the responsibilities that I was given so early on.

It had not been that long since I had become a Christian, but it seemed the fast forward button had been pushed due to the circumstances and surroundings of my life.

Within a year, I had become a leader at our church and at the Solid Rock Café. My enthusiasm was misinterpreted for maturity, so I was often asked to lead in Bible studies and talks. One night I talked about how rock music can be a form of Satan worship, and ended my sermon by stomping on some of my old music. I spent most of my talk reading lyrics from rock groups Nine Inch Nails and Metallica instead of verses from the Bible. Then, I told everyone that unless we listened to Christian music exclusively, we were filling our minds up with garbage. There was no room for compromise in my world.

Everything had to go. Within a few weeks, dozens of us had joined with another local church for a record and tape burning. We left that night so proud of our accomplishment. But once the flames died down, all we were left with were the ashes. A month later, I found a stack of non-Christian music tapes in a friend's carrying case. Without asking his permission, I destroyed the tapes. When he came into the room and found his music shredded to pieces, he furiously asked me why I had done what I did.

"It's wrong for you to have music like this. I'm doing it for your own good," I told him. I was actually proud. I was so busy gutting out my music (and everyone else's) that I failed to fill the now-empty spaces with God. Oh, how I wish I could have my old collector's edition U2 records back.

The Punch Club was another of my bright ideas. I was having trouble with cursing since I had spent most of my teenage years using inappropriate language to express my feelings. I needed help to stop, and felt compelled to enlist others to join in this crusade. So, I asked several others to join the Punch Club. The sole purpose of the club was to punch other club members in the arms as hard as possible when they were caught cursing. It started as a simple way to teach the principle that disobedience is usually followed by pain. But within a month, it had become less about accountability and more about wanting a Punch Club member to curse so you could hit them. A friend nailed you, and you were waiting for payback. Outwardly it was working, but in my mind I was cursing just as much. I walked around, bruised both physically and emotionally. When I cursed and a friend hit me, as requested, I'd say, "No, you don't understand. I want a bruise!" The exercise was less about being broken hearted for the language that broke the heart of God, and more about a fun testosterone-driven way to hit somebody.

I had escaped religion for the God of grace, but somehow found myself becoming the very thing I despised: a do-gooder who was mad all the time at any fellow Christian who didn't share my convictions.

I didn't realize that the same grace that had saved me was the grace that could sustain me. The Christians that had led me to the Lord were experts at explaining and extending the saving grace of the gospel. I knew that God loved me and had forgiven me of my sins, not because of what I had done, but because of what Jesus had done. On this side of the cross, however, I found myself no longer under its shadow. Maybe the reason none of my friends were teaching me how to pursue holiness without becoming a legalist was because they were struggling with that very concept themselves.

I realize now that my legalism was an overreaction to the legitimate detox work that needed to be done. Oh yes, I needed detox all right. The enemy's camp had been my hiding place for a long time. Now I'd gone over to the other side, but my mind hadn't caught up with my heart. Christ had given me a new identity, but I still had liabilities from the past. The rock music that had pickled my brain for years still clouded my head sometimes, and I continued to struggle with anger and lust issues. My cursing was way out of hand. When you go for years living life on your own terms, then all of a sudden Christ saves your heart, it can be a genuine shock to the system.

So much of my actions was symptomatic troubleshooting, rather than heart-changing obedience. Maybe for others, it was an actual waging of war in a pursuit for ultimate satisfaction found in Christ. But mine was based on fear.

Fear that I would go back to my old ways.

Fear that God was going to get me if I misbehaved.

Fear that I would be an ungodly leader if I didn't push people.

Although I wanted to do what was right, I wasn't doing it for the right reasons. It's too bad that at the very beginning of my journey with Christ somebody hadn't taught me a healthy lesson about fearing God. I'd thought of God as angry for so long, I expected he would be mad at me for cursing or having lustful thoughts. So I punished myself almost like Thomas Becket, the twelfth-century Archbishop of Canterbury who wore a hair shirt under his robes as a private penance to God. It was years into my Christian walk before I understood what the fear of God is all about, and that true fear of God is in fact a joy.

What I strained so hard to understand was that whether or not I used bad language, had unclean thoughts, won or lost any particular skirmish in my war against sin, Jesus was always there with me. He was never going to leave me. I thought I had a long checklist of religious behavior to go through so God would be pleased with me. I was afraid of what would happen if I didn't toe the line, so I cleaned up my act out of fear.

Jerry Bridges tells a story in his book *The Joy of Fearing God* that helped me turn a corner. The story is about a soldier whose job is driving a general around. He's always afraid he's going to get lost or do something wrong to make the general mad, so he's on edge all the time and worried about making a mistake. One day the soldier is in a bad accident, and when he wakes up in the hospital, the general is sitting beside him. The general gently takes care of the soldier and stays with him until he begins to heal, and the soldier loves him for his kindness and compassion. Even though the powerful, important general doesn't owe the soldier anything, he devotes his time and attention to this underling enlisted man who will probably never be able to repay such kindness. Once the soldier recovers, he goes back to driving the general around, but now he's doing it out of love and respect and thanksgiving, not out of fear.

Religion is all about the mean general who has power over you and scares you into obedience. Grace is about the love and unmerited forgiveness of God through Christ. Unlike my tendency at the time, a lot of people mistakenly believe grace means they can treat the general like their buddy and not have to be obedient to him or listen to his commands. That doesn't work, either. The soldier is still obedient to the general. But now he follows the general's orders out of love, because he knows in his bones how much the general loves him.

12

THE POWER
OF PARKING LOTS

Go get me a Coke. I want to talk with you."

It was a Saturday morning when my dad walked into my room with this command. I was a junior in high school, and in those days his coming to my room meant I was probably in trouble. My mind raced. *Which of my teachers called? Is it my grades? Did he find a joint?* My heart pounding, I went downstairs to the kitchen and opened the fridge. I couldn't find a Coke, so I got some orange juice instead and brought it back upstairs.

I skipped stairs, anxious to hear what my father wanted to discuss. "This is not a Coke," he said. I told him we didn't have any.

"Did I ask you if we have a Coke?"

"No, sir."

"Go get me a Coke!"

"You want me to get you a Coke that we don't have?"

"I want you to get me a Coke. I didn't ask you if we have any; I told you to get me one."

I got in the car and drove a mile and a half to the convenience store down the street to buy my father the Coke he apparently had to have.

Ten minutes later, as I entered my room with an ice-filled glass of fizzy soda, I found Dad sitting right where I left him. On my bed. Sitting, and waiting.

He took a sip and set it down.

"This is what I'm worried that you've become," he said, dead serious.

"What have I become?" I asked, relieved that this evidently had nothing to do with school or illegal substances. "You are becoming American," he declared. "I have noticed lately that every time I ask you for something, if it's not easy to get, you just say we don't have it or it's not available. This is not how I have raised you to think. I asked you to get me a Coke. You go and see we have no Coke, and you bring me no Coke. If we have no Coke, go get a Coke."

Then he got to the point. "If in life you stop at the first no, you'll never be anything more than average. The answer should always be yes; you are allowed a 'not yet,' but never a 'no' if you can help it. Tell yourself, 'I don't know how I'll make it happen, but I'll figure it out.' You need to decide that you're going to be a come-through kind of guy. You're going to win at everything you want to do in this world. Especially in this culture, where people see a speed bump and think it's a road block."

This was not the first time that I had received a thirty-minute lecture on the "American way" versus the "Iraninan way." I wanted to say, "Hey, if the Iranian ways are so much better, then why don't you just go back?" but I dared not. Actually, my parents used the "American way" line as a blanket statement that meant different things at different times. This time his comment was not rooted out of comparison of two different nations, but out of two different generations. You need more than an English to Persian dictionary to translate his thoughts. With my father, there is always what he says in English and then there is what he thought he was saying in English. This time, however, the message was very clear: think ahead and take initiative. In those days I saw these long discussions as a nusiance, but now I see them in a different light.

In Dad I had more than a father; I had a mentor. A Yoda that was willing to teach the young Jedi about the ways of the Force.

The tools he bestowed were those of the mind and wit. My father never taught me how to chop wood properly or how to change the oil in the car, but he did teach me how to hire the right man to get the job done. To this day, I have never met a more competent businessman. My father had mastered the art of negotiation, and I was fortunate to be his pupil.

Dad mentored me in every way he could, but what he couldn't do was be a spiritual father who mentored me in my walk with Christ. He was a great man, but not a Christian.

I needed mentorship and Christian fathering badly. Not just as a believer, but also as someone who was realizing that ministry was all I wanted to do. The more God was using me at such an early stage in my faith, the more I knew I needed training and mentorship.

Larry Noh, Allen Wilson, and a few others were helpful as leaders, but I needed a spiritual father. A man of God who would take me under his wing.

Enter Rick Stanley.

The first time I saw Rick Stanley was when he preached at Shades Mountain Baptist as a guest speaker.

I had never seen anything like him; he looked like a movie star. With his feathered long blond hair and over-the-top demeanor, Rick Stanley demanded your attention the minute he walked into a room. That morning, I heard a new kind of sermon, one with the same kind of biblical message as our pastor would give, but delivered with a different method.

Halfway through the message, I looked over to the row of guys in my pew and mouthed the words "Wow." Larry whispered in my ear, "This is the fifth time I've heard him. He is always this good."

Rick told his captivating story. How he grew up aban-
doned in a foster home, until one day his mother reappeared,
recently married to Vernon Presley, Elvis's widowed father.
That very afternoon, Rick and his brothers were taken to
Graceland. Living with Elvis changed everything. During his
teenage years Rick traveled with Elvis and eventually became
hooked on drugs and everything else imaginable. Because his
life revolved around Elvis and his rock 'n' roll lifestyle, Rick
saw everything come to a halt when Elvis died. The death of
The King was what God used to grab Rick's attention, and
eventually his heart.

At the end of the service, the pastor announced that Rick
was going to be the speaker at our church's summer youth
camp at the beach that June. The teenagers erupted in cheers.
I had already signed up to go as a counselor, and now Rick
was speaking. I couldn't wait till the night camp started.

Unfortunately, at the last minute, we received word he
wasn't going to make it that first night because he was ap-
pearing on *Larry King Live*. Instead of listening to him in
person, we all watched him on TV. He talked about growing
up at Graceland and about his faith. Larry King called him
one of the most in-demand evangelical speakers in the country, to which someone in the camp audience yelled "We've
got him all week!" Larry King was right. Rick was everywhere. *People* magazine had written an eight-page article
about Rick, and news of his radical conversion was getting
press everywhere, from *Good Morning America* to the *Dallas Morning News*.

Dad as a military student in training.

Mom and Dad when they were first engaged.

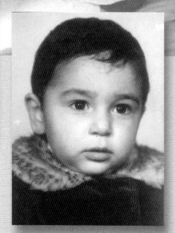

Our family. Taken the year of the revolution.

Me at the age of two.

Iranian Revolution demonstrators loot government bureaus and banks as well as liquor shops, cabarets, and cinemas during the Revolution in Tehran, November 4, 1978. Documents thrown out of the buildings are spread on the street while furniture is set ablaze.

Photo by Kaveh Kazemi/Getty Images

The Iranian Islamic Republic Army demonstrates in solidarity with people in the street during the Iranian Revolution. They are carrying posters of the Ayatollah Khomeini, the Iranian religious and political leader.

Photo by Keystone/Getty Images

At school in Iran. I'm in the front row, second from left.

The elementary school on the army base in Munich, Germany, where we waited to be allowed into the United States.

MUNICH
ELEMENTARY
SCHOOL
GERMANY 1980
MRS KRONMUELL'
GRADE 3

Nastaran and me wearing the dreaded lederhosen.

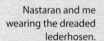

"Nasa." My birthday party in the garage.

Benjamin and me in 1986. My "geek-to-chic" days.

Dad at Café de France, his restaurant at the botanical gardens.

Craig Cosper and me winning a tennis doubles tournament in Dothan, Alabama in 1984.

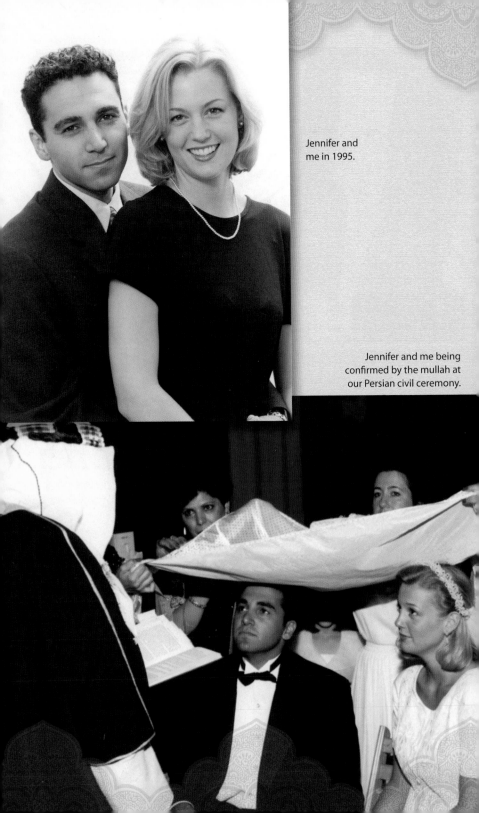

Jennifer and me in 1995.

Jennifer and me being confirmed by the mullah at our Persian civil ceremony.

Dr. Carter handing me my certificate of ordination at Shades Mountain Baptist.

Speaking at a Billy Graham Association crusade (Carbondale, IL, 1997).

The entire Nasser, Davis, and Morgan gang, taken the day our son, Rudy, came home from Guatemala.

Our family.

Our family in 2007. Top row from left: Dad, Mom, Benjamin, Cary. Middle row: David, Jennifer, Nastaran. Bottom row: Rudy, Simene, Grace, Emmanuel.

Rick got to our camp the second night. I was on the basketball court, and Rick was fresh off his flight from New York when I saw him walking toward us with Allen, our youth pastor. As he got closer, we all stopped playing basketball and walked over to say hi.

He was wearing cut-off khakis, a white T-shirt, and a safari vest. His vest was loaded down, as if he had just gotten back from Kilimanjaro. I could see through the mesh vent in one of his pockets that he carried a red Swiss Army knife, tucked in by a small Bible. His sunglasses were perched on top of his head, pulling back his long hair.

I thought, this guy is either trying way too hard, or being this cool is the most effortless thing he does. Without a hello or anything, Rick stopped and pointed at me. "I've heard about you."

"What?"

"I've heard a lot about you. David Nasser, right? Heard good things. I'm really excited about your being here. I want you to come and hang with me during this week. I want to get to know you better."

I was both fascinated and intimidated.

We started hanging out, and I realized the reason he had an interest in investing in me was because my pastor had told him he and I had a lot in common. There was a call on our lives to tell our stories, not for our sake, but to boast about the cross. Rick knew what it was like to have a testimony that was unusual. He knew the benefits of having a thrilling story to tell, but also the pitfalls. We were alike in a lot of ways.

If anyone understood what it was like to be the freak at the circus whom everyone wants to see, he did. He understood what it was like to have tons of money one day and to lose it overnight. He knew what it was like to have a military father who was a not a Christian. He knew what it was like to need a spiritual dad.

I loved his sermons that week, but what I really appreciated was who he was off stage. I remember his humility. He was so confident, but his confidence didn't come across as if he were a big deal at all. He was there to serve.

By the end of the week, Rick asked me if I would go on the road and travel with him as an intern. I couldn't say yes fast enough.

My ministry was to help him do better ministry. Internship meant doing the small stuff that made his life easier. I traveled with him as a source of accountability, and to keep him company. I set up and sold his ministry resources. We couldn't keep the books in stock. The sales of these items helped Rick to do ministry for a low cost to whatever church was hosting him. He called it his tent-making business. He explained that in the Bible, some of the disciples made tents to raise money for the necessities of life. Then they could keep surviving as they traveled and did ministry.

I learned a lot about selling books in those days. I learned from Rick how to give a ton of them away to anybody who wanted one, but couldn't afford it. I realize now that we sold so many because God was blessing Rick's giving spirit more than his entrepreneurial ability.

We talked a lot about preaching, and he answered every question I could throw at him. How do you develop a message? What is your favorite verse in the Bible to preach on and why? How do you incorporate illustrations in your sermons? We discussed less important topics as well, such as why wearing the color white on stage is a bad idea. Rick always patiently indulged my questions, no matter how deeply spiritual or ridiculously trivial.

Rick was a student of preaching. We traveled with Bible commentaries and lots and lots of tapes. Long trips in the van consisted of listening to sermon series from different pastors, with Led Zeppelin and Lynyrd Skynyrd breaks in between. Rick loved rock 'n' roll. He cranked the van speakers with '70s guitar riffs as if we were two teenagers in a red Mustang.

Months away from my record-burning past, I learned that you could love God with all your heart and still jam to "Sweet Home Alabama." When I told Rick what I had done with my old U2 and Metallica records, he laughed. "Some of that is junk you don't need, but you should have kept the U2, Bud." By the next week, he had given me every record U2 ever released.

I lived with Rick on the road, so I got to see and hear it all—from the long-distance phone dates with his wife, to stops at the mall to buy his daughters Malibu Barbies. I kept learning from him, sometimes learning how to be, and sometimes how not to be. One early morning, I saw Rick snap at a gate agent at the airport. She was rude, but so was he. When we got on the plane, Rick looked at me and apologized. He said, "I'm sorry, Bud. I'm just tired this morning, and so I just blew it with that lady. I wish I could turn this plane around and ask that rude lady back there to forgive me. Everyone is important to God, and we need to preach with our lives, not just our words, no matter what time it is." He meant it, because I saw him live it out during late-night Waffle House runs when he picked up the tab for strangers who seemed down and out.

It wasn't always Waffle Houses. We ate at some fancy steak houses as well. I remember getting to eat at an exclusive place with Rick and Dr. W. A. Criswell, the pastor of First Baptist Dallas and president of Criswell College. There I was, a nineteen-year-old kid, sitting with a great man of God, listening in as he poured into Rick. I watched my mentor get mentored that day. Rick always invited me to go and hang with the pastors and Christian bands that roamed the Christian music festival scene in those days. To Rick, I was never just a fly on the wall. He gave me access to well-known people in his circle of peers. If they didn't bring me into the conversation, he'd say, "You've got to hear what God has done in this young man's life. You won't believe it." I ate ice cream with Russ Taff and stayed up until four in the morning hanging out with DeGarmo and Key. These were bands that only the Christian subculture knew about, but through Rick, I also had brushes with big-time fame.

One day I was flipping channels in a hotel room while Rick was in the bathroom. He was taking a shower to get ready for the evangelistic service later that night. The phone rang, and I picked up.

"Hello."

"Yes, is Ricky there?" said a man with a thick British accent.

"I'm sorry. He is here, but he is taking a shower. I'm his intern. Can I take a message?"

"Yes, please tell him Eric called and that I am grateful for his prayers."

"Yes, sir." Click.

A few minutes later, when Rick got out, I gave him the message.

"It's so sad, isn't it, what happened to his son. I've been praying for him all week," Rick said.

Out of nowhere it hit me. I just took a call from Eric Clapton, whose four-year-old son had tragically died after falling fifty-three stories out of a window.

"That was Eric Clapton I just talked to on the phone? Are you kidding me?"

Rick just looked at me teary-eyed and said, "Yeah, we need to be praying for him and his family."

I began to realize that Rick's relation to Elvis meant he didn't just listen to Zeppelin. He hung out with them. He didn't just talk about the dangers of seduction in one of his sermons, he knew firsthand about its hooks, because he had hung out at Hugh Hefner's Playboy mansion. This guy had lived a crazy existence, and now, because of the calling on his life to be a preacher, and his desire to serve God, he was rooming with me at a Holiday Inn in the middle of nowhere.

The tuition for such mentorship was service. I wanted to serve Rick, because I realized what it cost him to serve the kingdom. My goal became trying to figure out a way to guess his needs and to meet them before he even asked. I was experiencing a major change in motive. I found that my relationship with Rick was teaching me how to serve God out of a spirit of gratitude and love, instead of an attitude of fear.

"We need to drop off my suit at the cleaners."

"Already did it this morning while you were having breakfast."

"Who washed and waxed the van?"

"I did, while you were taking a nap."

"Come and eat with us, David."

"No, I'll stay here and count out the resource inventory. Who wants to sit with two old guys as they talk about their old seminary days?"

I dropped the ball plenty as well. There were many times when I didn't do my best job, or I messed up on a responsibility, but Rick always used the opportunity to teach me something. One time, Rick sent me to ship some merchandise to the place where he was scheduled to speak in four days. He told me to ship for next-day delivery, but I forgot to take my wallet to the post office. So rather than drive thirty minutes to go back for my wallet, I went on a scavenger hunt in my car for loose change. My two handfuls of quarters and nickels were not enough to ship the product via next-day delivery, but I had enough for three-day delivery. Out of laziness, I took a risk, and sent them three-day. Guess what? The items didn't arrive until the morning we left, when we had to ship them right back. I cost the ministry a thousand dollars or more in lost sales. I could have blamed the post office, but I knew I was to blame, because I didn't do what Rick asked me to do. If I'd learned the lesson my dad tried to teach by sending me out for a Coke, I would never have made that mistake. It was an expensive lesson. Trust me, Rick made that clear, but he also forgave me.

That wasn't the only time, either. If I said something inappropriate in front of someone, I knew a rebuke was coming later when we were alone. But so was grace.

Elvis loved surprises, so Rick grew up watching his big brother surprise people with unexpected gifts. It wasn't unusual for Elvis to pull a pink Cadillac into someone's driveway and hand over the keys. Rick's favorite surprise for me, however, was the pulpit. At any random moment—he loved giving no warning—he'd bring me onstage and say, "David, why don't you share for a few minutes?" Sometimes it would be in front of thirty people, sometimes three thousand. I didn't know whether I'd have five minutes or fifteen, but I knew every minute needed to be filled with Christ-centered truth. That's how I learned to preach on the spot. Rick taught me that preaching needs to feel less like a speech and more like a conversation, no matter what the size of the audience.

One day we were in Texas so that Rick could speak at an evangelistic event hosted by Dr. Jay Strack. I had met so many great men and women through Rick, but none as impressive as Dr. Strack. Rick's friends were always kind to me, but Dr. Jay went above and beyond. For two days in a row he took me out for coffee and gave me as much time as I wanted to pick his brain. I was just a teenager who sold ministry resources for his friend, but he treated me like I was the son of a sultan. I wanted to write down everything Dr. Jay said. Rick called them "Jayisms"—little nuggets of truth that you can't get out of your head. "Jesus loves you just as you are, but he loves you too much to leave you that way," and "it's time for the little boy to sit down, and the man to stand up." I still remember them all.

By the end of that week, Rick told me Dr. Jay wanted me to speak for him at school assemblies and pre-crusade rallies all over the country.

"But I'm working for you," I said.

"You can still serve with me, but just once a month. It's time to take the training wheels off, Bud. Jay will only need you a few days a month, which will leave you time to be home in Birmingham more, and now you can say yes to your own speaking invitations." I was starting to receive invitations to speak, but up to that point I usually said no because I was focused on helping Rick.

"Do you think I'm ready?"

"You're willing and you're learning, Dave. That's all any of us can do. Besides, I recommended you to Jay, so you better not let me down," he said, laughing.

And so for the next two years, I spent an average of two or three days a month serving under Dr. Jay. I was beginning to speak more and more on my own. After a year or so, I didn't get to see these two men as much as before, but they were always a phone call away.

When I asked Shades Mountain Baptist to license me as a minister, staff member Aubrey Edwards said yes, on the condition that I would clean up my appearance. He asked that I cut my hair and quit wearing jeans with holes in them. I was offended and saw it as legalism. Aubrey had been the very person who had ministered to my dad at his restaurant. Without him, my father would never have allowed me to go to church in the first place. More than anybody else from that church, he had invested in my father. I owed so much to this man, but my hair was what he wanted? I was upset, but when I called Jay, he set me straight.

"What Aubrey Edwards is asking of you is not really about hair and fashion, David. This is about submission. Your church is watching to see how you react to these little tests. Aubrey wants to see if you're willing to give up some of your rights and are willing to make sacrifices for the greater good. Is long hair a sin? I hope not, because Jesus probably had long hair, but not falling under authority is a sin. What do you want more, long hair, or to be licensed from your church?"

The next day, I got my hair chopped off. Within a few months, my hair had grown long again, and no one complimented me on it more than Aubrey. This man of God taught me that in all of life, not just ministry—in friendships, marriage, and anything else worth being a part of—you have to be willing to give up your rights for the good of the relationship. He wasn't asking me to compromise on my convictions, just my hair length.

I have a hunch that Aubrey, Jay, and Rick must have had a few phone conversations behind my back about where this young preacher needed pruning and shaping once in a while. If so, I am even more thankful for their investment.

As the years have passed, I have had the blessing of knowing other great men who have served as mentors to me. There was Franklin Graham, who let me be a part of the Billy Graham Evangelistic Team for more than a hundred events. There have also been other men—Dr. Charles Carter, Fenton Moorehead, Jim Jackson, Perry Dugger, Rick Ousley, and my pastor today, Buddy Gray—who have poured prayers, Scripture, and advice into my life.

Then there were laypeople who were not in official ministry roles but still cared for me like a child who needed help growing up. Dale Bynum taught me many things, but none more powerful than a love for theology. His dining room had been converted into a library, filled to the brim with Spurgeon, Dagg, Calvin, and Augustine. He gave me permission to read his books, but he demonstrated to me the theology in their pages through his life.

I even had spiritual fathering from a man whom I have talked to for no more than two minutes my whole life. After a few years of doing ministry, just about everyone in my life agreed that I needed to go to college. By that time I was so busy doing ministry that I didn't want to slow down, but one of Dr. Strack's "Jayisms" was "Never allow ministry to get in the way of preparation for ministry." I listened, but knew that I didn't have enough money to pay for college.

One early morning, the phone rang in the apartment. A lady I had never met told me that she was a Christian who knew about my need for schooling, and she had been praying for me. She asked if I would go to Green Valley Baptist Church and wait at the front parking lot for a man in a truck.

The request was awkward, but I was intrigued, so I nervously agreed to it. She gave me directions, and I realized that the church was only ten minutes from my apartment. I told her I could be there in less than half an hour.

Thirty minutes later, I was sitting in my car when a man in a big pickup truck pulled in the spot beside me. He looked like a contractor or someone who worked with his hands. Think John Wayne meets Bob the Builder. We both got out and walked over to one another.

"David?"

"Yes, sir."

"I'm Mr. Russell. Thanks for coming out here on such short notice to meet me. I was told you could use a little help with college tuition. Here you go, son."

He reached into his jacket pocket and pulled out an envelope bearing my name, misspelled: "David Nassier."

"There's a check in there big enough to pay your tuition for one year of college."

I was speechless. "Thank you, sir," I stammered, standing there like a deer in the headlights.

"Sure, son. I'll be praying for you." He seemed uncomfortable with being thanked, so he stepped away, got in his truck, and drove off, waving as he left.

I stood there in the parking lot crying. What was it with me and parking lots? First the Shoney's incident, then the eighty-three-dollar incident, and now this. *I should hang out in parking lots more often!*

At the risk of jumping too far ahead in my story, just a few months ago, I was standing in line at an equipment rental place to check out a cotton candy machine for my little girl's birthday party. A white-bearded man stood in front of me in line. He looked familiar, but I couldn't place him. As his turn came to talk to the store employee, I overheard his voice, and it sounded familiar. *Who is this guy?*

"See you tomorrow, Mr. Russell," said the man behind the counter.

Mr. Russell turned around and smiled at me, but he had no idea who I was.

"May I help you, sir?" the rental agent said.

I stood there in awe for a few moments, then shook my head no and walked quickly to the parking lot.

"Mr. Russell?" I called out, as he was just about to close the door to his truck.

"Yes?"

"Mr. Russell, you don't remember me, sir, but I sure remember you. Sir, about twenty years ago, you and I met for about thirty seconds in the parking lot of Green Valley Baptist

Church. You stepped out of your truck and walked into my life, sir, with a gift. A gift that helped me grow as a minister. You paid for my school. Do you remember that?"

He looked at me, and his eyes lit up. "I remember you now, son. What can I do for you?"

"Nothing, Mr. Russell, I just wanted to say thanks for what you've already done. I'm a minister now, a husband, and a father. I travel all over the world speaking, and I've authored four books so far. I don't say any of this to brag, sir, just to let you know that you sowed a seed that has been fruitful in God's kingdom."

He teared up a little. "David, what can I do for you now? Do you need anything I can help you with?"

His humility and servant's heart mentored me again right then and there. Once again, in a parking lot, I found myself lavished with grace.

13

RISK AND ROMANCE

By the summer of 1991, I was juggling school, speaking, and interning all at once. The Solid Rock Café had shut down due to lack of funds. With it had gone our apartment.

Thanks to Mr. Russell, I was able to enroll at the University of Montevallo, where my sister attended. Montevallo is a small Southern town much like Enterprise, with the exception that it's only thirty miles from the big city of Birmingham. Just far enough not to be a suburb, but close enough that I could commute. It was at Montevallo's meeting of Campus Crusade for Christ that I met fellow believers Robie Sarkar and Lance Elliot. Lance was the musical type, trendy, creative, and not afraid to go against the grain. I had never met someone with so much talent and such diverse musical tastes. The first time we met, Lance told me he was writing techno music with Christian lyrics. At first glance, Robie couldn't have been more different. He wore flannel shirts and looked like an L.L.Bean ad. Robie was charismatic and winsome. Every day after class, his goal was to go rock climbing or mudding. Despite our diversity, or maybe because of it, the three of us hit it off instantly and became joined at the hip. By the end of the year, we had moved in together into a small loft in downtown Birmingham.

Our loft was a far cry from my old apartment. It had high ceilings, wide plank floors, and windows that let sunlight fill the rooms. Rent, tuition, and the everyday expenses of life were no longer an issue. I was a single guy who was traveling and speaking on the weekends, and that meant that I brought home a check just about every week. Robie's parents were both doctors, and Lance's dad owned a large irrigation company. All that to say, we had a lot of fun "bachelor padding" our loft with oversized speakers and black furniture. Although these carefree college days were short-lived for me, I look back on them now with such fondness. I was so busy responding to speaking requests that summer, I could only intern for Rick at one camp. I'm so glad I was free that week, and in the pages ahead you'll find out why.

The life journeys that brought Jennifer Davis and David Nasser together during that youth camp all those years ago could not have been more different. Mine was a life filled with unexpected twists and turns, while Jennifer had lived a safe, predictable upbringing where Mom was an elementary school teacher and Dad was a trusted church member who helped take the offering every Sunday. I had a scandalous past filled with dangerous sin; Jennifer had lived a sheltered existence and graduated summa cum laude from high school and college.

We also looked as different as night and day. Jennifer was the picture of an all-American girl, sandy-blond hair and a smile perfected by years of devotion to a retainer. She looked like a model from the J. Crew catalog. I looked like a cover boy for *National Geographic!*

We were both fairly new believers, wanting God to use us that week. Jennifer had grown up in church, but at the age of sixteen, at an evangelistic event, she realized that even though she was a leader in her church, she had never really received the redemptive power of the gospel. Up to that point, her life had been filled with good behavior and great intentions, but that had only resulted in her being religious, not redeemed. When Jennifer told her church she had not been a Christian, they said she was wrong. They reminded her that she was a very good person, but Jennifer had been awakened to the truth that Christianity is not about bad people becoming good. It's about dead people becoming alive.

Her path was one of repentance from self-righteousness, while the road I traveled was one of repentance from unrighteousness. But ultimately, both journeys had brought us to the foot of the cross. The two of us had been delivered from the destructive fires of religion and into the arms of grace.

Jennifer and I certainly hadn't traveled to Lookout Mountain, Georgia looking for love, much less each other, but in hindsight, Covenant College was a very romantic spot to meet.

The campus straddles the ridge along the Georgia–Tennessee line, where generations of tourists have come to "see seven states," as local tradition has it. The main building was originally a hotel that opened in the roaring '20s for wealthy socialites and was frequented by such movie stars as Elizabeth Taylor. Covenant College has been on site there since the 1960s, allowing its surroundings to be a retreat-like environment for generations of students. The chapel is filled with stained glass that could rival an old Catholic church in Ireland. It is a perfect place for churches to hold youth camps during summer break. For Jennifer and me, it will always be more than simply a great location for camp.

That particular week, we were among seven hundred other participants at Summit Camp, a combined effort of thirty or so churches to minister to teenagers. Jennifer was there for the week to serve as a counselor. For her, this was a way to serve while on summer break as a junior at the University of Alabama. I had driven there to help Rick in any way he needed.

The teenagers at the camp were divided into "family groups," each with a male and female counselor ("mom" and "dad") assigned to it. Jennifer served as one of those moms, and due to a last-minute need for a substitute, I became one of the dads. It's ironic when I look back now that before we even set eyes on one another, someone put us together to lead a family.

As we met twice a day with our family group to discuss what God was doing in our lives, I watched Jennifer lead with compassion and authenticity. The "mom" role had forced her to be very out-loud about her faith, exposing her deep-rooted understanding of Scripture and commitment to God. I was smitten. It didn't hurt that she was drop-dead gorgeous. Jennifer and I got along great that week as we ministered to our temporary family, but it was obvious she only saw me as a new friend and nothing more.

After all, she did have a boyfriend.

As a matter of fact, he was at camp that week too. He served as "dad" for another family group. I saw him sitting with Jennifer the first night of camp in the chapel, and realized that this couple cared for each other. Her boyfriend seemed like an awesome guy, the kind who was interested in being the best possible counselor and example for these teenagers. The two of them looked good as a couple, and I prayed that God would one day allow me to be as lucky as that guy. I would be lying if I said I wasn't interested in her at first, but when I knew they had been a couple for four years, and he was the only guy she had ever dated, I quickly put any thoughts of a connection to rest. I left the camp that week thinking that she would probably be engaged within a few months.

Fast-forward 365 days later. Jennifer and I unexpectedly met again in the main lobby of Covenant College. She was back at Summit Camp as a counselor, and I was back with Rick. But this time I was also the morning speaker.

After exchanging hellos and some small talk about how college life was for her and how I'd moved around that year in order to learn more about ministry, I mustered up the courage to ask if she was still with her old flame. I asked if he was at the camp too, assuming the two of them were still together.

"Yes, we're still together," she affirmed, "but he couldn't get off work to be here."

We exchanged goodbyes and went our separate ways.

During the rest of the week, we saw each other here and there. Covenant is a tiny campus, so running into her was not hard to do. And to add to it, Jenn was asked to volunteer to help sell resources for Rick, since I had to speak in the mornings. This gave us even more hang time.

On the last day of camp, all seven hundred participants piled into buses and vans to go white-water rafting on the Ocoee River. This was a camp tradition and a fun way to end the week. I asked Jennifer if we could ride together to the Ocoee, because I had a question that I really needed to ask her. She hesitated, but said yes, and ten minutes later we were sitting side by side on our way down the mountain.

"Jennifer, I realize this is really awkward, but I want you to know that I thought about you last year when I was reading a particular book."

She looked puzzled. "What book?"

"It's called *The Bridges of Madison County*. Have you heard of it?"

I knew she had. Everyone had. It quickly became one of the best-selling novels of all time. Rumor had it that Hollywood was going to turn this love story into a movie starring Clint Eastwood and Meryl Streep. Robert James Waller's short, tragic tale was about Francesca Johnson, a farm wife living quietly in Madison County, Iowa, who was born in Italy and came to America as a war bride. Francesca feels content enough with life, until one day, while her family is away for a few days, she meets Robert Kincaid. He is a free-spirited photographer looking for a covered bridge in her little town that he's supposed to shoot for *National Geographic*.

"I haven't read it," Jennifer said.

"I have read it," I replied. "I wanted to see why millions of people were buying this book. Understanding what about the story resonated with our culture could help me minister to people more effectively. I can't stand preachers who talk about something cultural that they don't know anything about. The book is definitely not Christian. It's a secular book with secular ideas, many of which I don't agree with; but in my opinion, it does ask one overarching question that might explain why so many people feel connected to it. That question is what brought you to my mind when I read it."

"Okay, ask away."

"Before I do, I want you to know that I have prayed about asking you this, and I feel like I am actually asking something God would want anyone to have asked of them."

This was a question that two friends, whether guys or girls, should be able to ask each other. As little as I knew about her, I'd figured out that most of her life, she'd been taught that the safest bet is the best one. I told her about how in *The Bridges of Madison County* the main character lives a life filled with regret, because she settled for a good man instead of the right man. I explained that in my opinion, people were not reading it by the truckload because they wanted to cheat on their spouses, or because they wanted to have an affair. I believed most people read it because they could relate to someone who gave up on their passions and dreams, because it was just easier to do what looked safe.

I didn't think Jennifer would end up like Francesca, but what I was pondering was an important question. Forget *Bridges of Madison County*; this question is all throughout the Bible. From Jesus asking a fisherman to drop his nets—a security blanket if ever there was one—to him putting the same choice before Paul, who left a well-respected scholar's job to become a slave for Christ, the question comes up again and again. It's in the story of the rich young ruler and the incredible saga of a teenage girl named Mary who didn't want to play it safe by saying, "No God, I don't want you to deliver your baby through me. I just want a normal, quiet, predictable life." It was a question I certainly needed asked of me, and a question that I felt I needed to ask her.

"Jennifer, when it comes to living out the rest of your life, are you looking for contentment, or are you looking to be overwhelmed?"

"What do you mean?"

133

"I mean, don't become a teacher just because everyone in your family did. That was their path, but does that overwhelm you? Is that what you want? What God wants for you?

"Are you and your boyfriend overwhelmed with each other, or is being together just the safe thing to do? This isn't about dating, or a job, but about living life with no regrets. Whoever you end up with, or whatever you end up doing with your life, I just want to encourage you to make sure it makes your heart beat fast. I'm not asking you out, Jennifer, or asking you to change your major at college, I'm just challenging you to make sure you don't end up living a life filled with regret. God's plans are not always the safest."

Jennifer just stared at me, momentarily speechless. I could tell I had made her feel uncomfortable.

She looked at me and simply said, "I'm with him, and that's where I want to be."

"Fair enough. I just thought someone needed to ask."

We sat there in silence, not knowing what else to say.

When we got to the Ocoee, we said our good-byes as we climbed aboard different rafts. Watching as the river carried her further and further away, I thought, *This is the last time I'm ever going to see that girl.*

I was so wrong.

Fast-forward another year. This time I wasn't at Covenant College, but I was serving as the summer youth speaker at a camp held at Judson College in Alabama. On the third night of the camp, some friends from out of town came to hear me speak. As we were wrapping up the service, I saw my friends slip out the back of the auditorium, and I ran to catch them in the parking lot. They'd already left, but I saw a man outside I thought was Al Elmore, the youth pastor who ran the camp and had invited me. Instead, it turned out to be his younger brother Eddie. He said everybody got the two of them mixed up, and I'm sure glad I did.

I hadn't met Eddie before, so as we walked back to the auditorium, I asked him where he was from. He said he lived in Northport, Alabama, and that he had driven down for the afternoon to spend a few hours with his brother. As soon as he said Northport, I thought of Jennifer's church.

"Where do you go to church?" I asked.

"Northport Baptist."

"Man, I know your church. I was at youth camp with your students the last two years. What a great church. I know it sounds weird, but there is a girl I met from your church that God really used to reveal some of the qualities I want in a wife someday. She—"

He interrupted me, mid-sentence. "You're talking about Jennifer Davis, aren't you?"

I was amazed. "Yes. How did you know?"

"Oh, lots of guys think she is great. It's a funny thing you should mention her," Eddie went on, "because I just found out Jennifer and her boyfriend broke up last week."

Broke up! My heart started pounding. I had to get in touch with her. I told Eddie that our meeting in this parking lot was a divine intervention. (If only he knew about my history with parking lots!) Eddie didn't have her phone number, but he took down mine. Within the next twenty-four hours, I called every Davis in Northport that the operator had a number for, but no luck.

Then, a couple of days later, she called me. Eddie, realizing God had placed him in that parking lot for a reason, had seen her at church and told her I wanted to talk. I was so happy to hear her voice. I was speaking the next weekend at a youth camp on the Alabama gulf coast, so I invited her to bring some friends and come down for the weekend session. I asked the youth pastor if it was okay for me to have a guest, and he helped me get Jennifer and her friends a place to stay.

I was so excited when they arrived. That night, after the service, five of us—Jennifer, her two friends, the worship leader from the camp, and I—went out to dinner. Afterward, we went for a walk on the beach together. Jennifer told me how thrilled she was to be getting her degree as a special education teacher. She wanted to enable children with special needs to flourish in school. She was so ready to graduate! We also talked about the direction that God was taking me. I told her about the things I had been learning, the places I had been to lately. By the end of our walk on the beach, I knew I was ready to pursue this girl with all of my heart.

People often ask me when I knew that Jennifer and I would end up together, and the answer is always the same: that night when we walked on the beach. I don't know if you could call it a first date, since there were five of us there and we were at a youth camp, but whatever you call it, it was the moment that I knew Jennifer would be my wife.

For Jennifer, things were a little more complicated. There was definitely a mutual attraction, and she loved my zeal for the Lord; but I was still an unproven, foreign-born, dark-skinned guy with a future that was a blank slate. There was no telling where my call to ministry would take me. An inner-city slum? Africa? Compared to her previous boyfriend, she and I had spent only a little time together. For years, her parents had assumed he would be their son-in-law. Upsetting their expectations was another risk. Dating me was way out of her comfort zone, but Jennifer was brave enough to venture in.

For both of us, this was about obedience. God was up to something special, and we wanted to see where it led.

There were still lots of other questions that needed answers: What makes you laugh? What makes you cry? What makes you scared? Do you like licorice? What makes you gag? (Never mind, I already asked the licorice question.) Are you a clean freak, or a slob? Do you like cats? Are you a night owl or a morning person? What do you think about kids? What about adoption? What are your convictions about raising children? What's your family really like? Can I live with this person? Can I live without this person?

Plus a million other little questions. And, of course the big one. The only one that really matters when it comes down to it: God, is this the person who will make me love you more?

A month later, I was sitting in my apartment one afternoon when the phone rang. I picked it up.

"Hello?"

"Grammy died."

Jennifer and I had been dating a little over a month when her grandmother passed. As soon as I heard the news, I drove the hour to Northport. Pulling into her grandparents' house, I realized I was mourning, not because I knew Mrs. Anders, but because I had fallen in love with her granddaughter. Sharing the pain of loss with Jennifer was not optional. Our hearts had become one, and if her heart was broken, so was mine. I knew that I had fallen in love with her a while back, but didn't want to pressure her with such a big declaration.

I got out of the car and started up the stairs to the back door. I had been there before and knew that was the door they always used. Before I got all the way up the stairs, Jennifer burst through the door and tearfully embraced me on the second step.

"I love you."

No "thanks for coming," no "I'm glad you're here as a shoulder to cry on," none of that. Instead, the girl who always waited and played it safe was making the declaration I was too afraid to make.

"I love you, too," I whispered. "I'm so sorry about your loss."

The next few days were filled with all the responsibilities that come when the life of a close family member ends. From making funeral arrangements and preparing for the settling of her estate to making sure the electric bill got paid, Jennifer's parents, aunt, and uncle rallied together to help. As friends and family paraded through to offer condolences or assist in any way possible, I realized Jennifer was well rooted in her

Northport community. Dozens upon dozens of people there knew her from the days when she was a child. I met many of them for the first time at either the memorial service or the funeral.

Most important was Jennifer's granddaddy, who was somewhat confused at what was happening around him. For years, Grammy had taken care of him, and now she was gone. He had been the healthier one physically, but she was the one whose mind had remained razor sharp. I remember just sitting with him while everyone was busy making arrangements.

"What's gonna come of me now?" he would ask periodically.

Jennifer's mother would hear him in the kitchen and come in from the living room to offer comfort. "Daddy, we're going to take good care of you. Don't you worry," she assured him with her warm Southern accent. As she hugged her elderly father and kissed him on the top of his head, I realized what a gift it must be to have your children around one day to take care of you in moments like that. My own mother never had that chance. She never got to say good-bye to her parents before they passed, because they were in Iran and we were in America. She was the only child in the family who was not there at the end. My father had seen both his parents pass before the revolution, but my mother had always hoped that one day she would get to see Maman-Gollé's face again. Her name translates to "the mother of all flowers," a fitting name for someone who was always as bright as a dozen red roses but as gentle as forget-me-nots. For my mother, the chance to return to Iran one day was not about getting her old house and stature back as much as getting to kiss the head of her mother, and holding her sister's hand when Maman-Gollé passed.

On the day of Grammy's funeral, Mrs. Davis asked me to give Granddaddy a haircut so that he would look presentable. I trimmed his thick, silvery hair and shaved his face and neck with his old lather brush, shaving cream, and razor. This was probably one of many personal things Grammy did for him every day. Who trimmed his nose hairs, and made sure his ears were cleaned out with a Q-tip? Who fixed his breakfast in the morning, washed his clothes, and whatever else had to be done? This was what love looked like in the twilight years.

Granddaddy had just lost the love of his life, while I had just found mine. As I ran a comb through his hair and helped him with his tie, I silently prayed for both of us. I prayed I would be just like him one day, outliving Jennifer. Not so that I could live longer, but so that she would never have to wonder who was left to hold her hand in her final hours. I prayed that Jennifer would never have to ask, "What's gonna come of me now?"

14

FIVE MONTHS

o let me get this right. You've been a Christian for a while now and decided to keep it quiet?" I didn't know whether to be mad or ecstatic.

I hadn't even come to her room to talk about Christ. I was there to ask her for a loan, so I could get my car fixed—and she just dropped the news on my lap as if she was talking about the weather.

I had been a Christian for five months, and things with Mom and Dad had been strained to say the least. My sister had certainly been sympathetic, but I just assumed she was being sweet, hoping I would denounce Christianity and come back to Islam. Little did I know, God had been chiseling away at her heart.

In her secret struggle with faith, she came to the conclusion that no matter what the problem is, Christ is the answer. Always the skeptic, Nastaran had gone about her examination of Christianity in a systematic way. The more she studied, the more she read, and the more she asked, the more she realized Jesus was more than a prophet. He is God.

As she told me about her decision to surrender her life to Christ, I wondered when she would break the news to Mom and Dad.

"Rather than making an announcement," she said, "I was hoping they would see Jesus in my life, that they would ask me what's so different. I know I don't live at home anymore, but whenever I'm around, I want Christ to shine his light through me. Don't worry, the chance will come, and when it does, I won't be silent."

She always was the smarter one!

Five months later, my mother called me to see if we could meet for lunch. She wanted to tell me some exciting news. Mom and I met for many lunches together in those days. The only rule Mom had when we met was that I not dress *lottee pootee*, which meant "like a vagabond," and that I shave and look presentable. "I don't want any of my friends to see me with you if you have jeans with holes in them. And no baseball hat. Remember, you are not *lottee pootee*." To Mom, appearance was very important. It didn't matter how much I told her that holes in jeans were actually the latest fashion. To her, it was slacks and ironed shirts, or nothing.

It was the norm for Mom and I to begin our lunches with small talk, catching up on what had been going on lately in her life and mine. This time, before we could even begin our usual conversation, she abruptly made an announcement, "I have to tell you now . . . I love Jesus too." My jaw dropped. She paused to let it sink in and then continued, "Jesus came to me in a dream and held my hand. We walked and talked together." As she was telling me this, I tried to picture that image. My beautiful, elegant mother who is always dressed like she is about to present a high society award at a ladies' luncheon, walking hand in hand with my bearded, rough-robed king. I wondered who did most of the talking. Was my mother giving fashion tips to the Savior, or was she speechless as he told her that he is her only hope?

She told me she believed Jesus was the Son of God because he told her he was. She had surrendered her heart to him. I wondered if Jesus had spoken to her in Persian or in English. She certainly thinks in Persian, since that is her native tongue. The thought seemed odd to me at first. An Iranian-looking Jesus that didn't speak in King James Bible English? But then I realized that the Jesus of the Bible spoke a language that was much closer to Persian than English, and he certainly looked more Middle Eastern than the Caucasian Jesus pictures we often see here in the States.

I called Nastaran to tell her the good news about Mom, but the quiet thunder had already rolled. She and Mom had been talking about the Lord for weeks.

One of the sweetest memories I will ever have came not too long after Mom's conversion. It was Christmas Eve and Dad had given me permission to come and stay at home during holiday break. I woke up at around four o'clock in the morning because I was thirsty. As I walked downstairs to the kitchen, I saw that the light in my parents' sunroom was on. Mom was sitting on the white leather sofa, wearing a white flowing sleeping gown, reading a white Bible with gold lettering. She looked angelic. As I walked closer and my sleepy eyes started to adjust to the light better, I noticed that the Bible pages were spotted with drops of water.

Then I saw a teardrop fall onto the page.

"Mom, what's wrong? Are you okay?"

"I can't believe I've waited so long to read this book."

I walked over and sat beside this extraordinary woman I was proud to call my mother. I had seen her cry the tears of a revolution, and the tears of loneliness, but now they were tears of redemption and joy. I gave her a hug. She smelled as beautiful as she looked. Trésor. Her signature scent. After a few moments of prayer together, I went back upstairs to go to bed, realizing God had woken me up to give me my Christmas gift early.

Next was Benjamin, and, you guessed it, his decision to become a Christ-follower came five months after my mother's.

For Benjamin, there was no rebellious struggle or religious pride. Mom, Nastaran, and I had been talking to him about the gospel, but because he has Down syndrome and God has created him in such a special way, it just took a little longer.

We certainly didn't want to force anything on him and realized that this was a decision he had to make himself. We just fasted and prayed that God would save him.

I was out of town speaking when Benjamin became a Christian, and I wondered if he really understood what being a worshipper of Jesus was all about. About two months after his conversion, he definitely showed me he knew more about worship than I did! His relationship with Christ was real and genuine.

On Father's Day, I arrived at the Birmingham airport after a weekend speaking event. If I hurried, I could catch most of the last service at Shades Mountain, so I got my luggage and drove to the church as fast as I could. The service had already started, so I slipped in the back and sat in an empty spot by myself.

Dr. Carter was standing behind the cross-shaped pulpit, welcoming everyone to the church, wishing the fathers in the room a happy Father's Day. Then out of nowhere, I saw Benjamin standing on the front left side of the sanctuary. I was in the back row, all the way to the right. I didn't even know that he was at church that morning, but Mom had brought him.

With everyone seated, it was surprising to see Ben out of his seat, walking right up to Dr. Carter. When he arrived at the pulpit, Ben reached into the inside pocket of his blazer and pulled out a red rose. The packed house of twenty-five hundred attendees, including Dr. Carter, silently stared in wonder as Ben proceeded to put the flower at the foot of the cross-shaped pulpit. He turned to the crowd and proudly proclaimed, "Happy Father's Day, Jesus!" With the room still in disbelief, Ben walked back to his seat as if nothing out of the ordinary had happened.

The guy sitting next to me leaned over and whispered. "Isn't that your brother?" I nodded yes, embarrassed. But to my surprise, the man said, "That was one of the most touching things I've ever seen. We should all be that in love with Jesus."

He was right. For the next few minutes, I sat there thinking about what I had just witnessed. I thought about how Ben must have premeditated the entire plan. How did he break free from Mom? Where did he get the rose? Did he have to cut its stem short enough to fit his pocket?

A few minutes later, when Dr. Carter stood to deliver his sermon, he made mention of Benjamin's thanksgiving offering as a sweet gesture that we all could learn from.

Benjamin's outward expression on Father's Day served as a reminder that everyone in my family had now become a Christian . . . except Dad. I wondered if that day would ever come.

15

Dad

Five months after I had become a Christian, Nastaran converted. Five months after that, Mom converted. Five months after that, Benjamin converted. But five years had passed since I became a Christian, and my father had yet to give his heart to the Lord.

In those five years, my relationship with Dad had become a roller coaster of emotions. After the first few years of wanting nothing to do with me, Dad started to warm up a bit. After all, he did love me. Sure his pride had been hurt, but I think he genuinely missed me since we barely saw each other in those days. Also, I assumed he was being nicer to appease Mom. He loved her so much, and if she was happier as a Christian, and she wanted to see her son more, he was willing to put up with me for her sake. In the fourth year, he even fixed up the basement of his home and allowed me to move back in.

I was a twenty-four-year-old preacher by that time, and I was able to live on my own, but moving back in meant that Dad and I could work on our relationship.

Dad and I seldom talked about Christianity, because we knew the subject would set off fireworks. He would make fun of the way I said "God" or chuckle at something Benjamin said about church, as if to say all this Jesus stuff was beneath him.

I admit that I was so busy in those days speaking all over the country that I missed opportunities to serve my father. He constantly complained that I didn't help enough at the restaurant and that his son was too busy for the family business. Frankly, he was right. I should have managed my time better. I should have said no to a few church invitations in order to stay home and spend more time with my family. They needed me, and I needed them, but I was too distracted sometimes to see that. Everywhere I went, I would ask people to pray for my father's conversion, while failing to realize that I could be a more effective missionary to my own father if I spent more time with him. I was busy building a ministry and pursuing Jennifer. Ministry and Jennifer were gifts God had bestowed on me, but I could have been a more helpful son.

One person who helped my relationship with Dad was Jennifer. Dad really liked her. She won him over with her warm personality and kindness. Throughout my life, Dad told me I needed to marry a good Iranian girl someday. But once Jennifer came into the picture, he quickly changed his tune. I started noticing that when Jennifer came around, my father came around. If she was at the house visiting, Dad would come and sit with us, bringing her a plate of peeled oranges and a glass of his perfectly blended cardamom tea in a tiny glass. From the very start, both Mom and Dad treated Jennifer as if she was their daughter. It was obvious they wanted me to marry this girl. When I kidded with my dad, saying that I thought he always wanted me to marry an Iranian girl, he replied with his thick accent, "She is so wonderful, I think she must be Iranian."

I was receiving the same warm welcome from Jennifer's parents. Sure, her father's very first words to me were "you're dark" as I walked into his house, but that, along with the fact that he was cleaning his shotgun during our entire first encounter, was more wit than anything else. Richard and Rebecca Davis had grown up only a couple of blocks from each other in their small Alabama town. Neither had ever traveled outside the United States, nor had their parents before them. Their lives were pretty contained, and they both found great comfort and stability in that. All that said, the thought of anyone in their family, let alone their only daughter, marrying a foreigner, was an idea they had never even entertained. I may never know what conversations took place behind closed doors at the Davis home, but obviously God was working in their hearts. And while Jennifer's parents didn't peel oranges when I went over to their house for a visit, and the tea was iced instead of hot, her mom made a mean peach cobbler with homemade ice cream.

While the Davises had grown to love me, and my parents had obviously embraced Jennifer, a burning question remained.

Would our parents like each other?

The Davises and the Nassers could not have been more different, but our hope was that the common bond of their kids being in love would be enough to bring them together. Jenn and I were so nervous the night they met. We actually got on our knees and begged God to hold our hands through what could potentially be a wildfire of cultural, religious, and personality divisions.

To our relief, the night couldn't have gone better. Mom put out her finest china and silver, and Dad grilled the biggest steaks we had ever seen. It was a celebration of unity. Two families that knew it would only be a matter of time before their children were walking side-by-side down a wedding aisle.

After dinner, Mr. Davis told us all he was going in for open-heart surgery the following week. Benjamin, never one to miss an opportunity for dramatic expression, insisted that we pray over Mr. Davis, and so we all gathered by the front door and closed our eyes. Everyone but my dad prayed out loud. I could hear Mr. Davis sniffling when Benjamin prayed his simple yet powerful words.

Little did we know that in less than a week, more than one heart would need God's healing.

Mr. Davis came through his quadruple bypass with flying colors. The doctors said the recovery would be slow for sure, but soon his heart would be healthier than ever. I was visiting him at the hospital, when Nastaran called to tell me she had been with Mom all day at the Kirklin Clinic.

"What's wrong?" I asked.

"Mom had chest pains last night, and so Dad took her to the emergency room. After some tests today, they have determined she needs open-heart surgery as soon as possible."

Could this be happening? Mr. Davis was not even out of the hospital from his surgery, and now we had my mother going under the knife as well?

We had escaped from Iran by saying we needed to leave for my mother to have heart surgery; now, fourteen years later, the truth had caught up with us.

The diagnosis was that Mom needed several bypasses and a valve replacement. She wasn't as strong as Mr. Davis, and the operation was a bit more severe, so we faced the real possibility that she would not make it. The doctors made it clear that if we had anything we needed to say to her, now was the time.

The morning of Mom's bypass surgery, I found myself in a hospital room full of dressed-up Iranians and ornate flowers. The room looked like a botanical garden, because every Iranian friend who came to lend support brought enough flowers to decorate a Rose Bowl float.

I had called a few minister friends to have them pray, but I made the mistake of forgetting to tell them not to come to the hospital. At the end of their visit, my friends asked if they could pray for Mom, and during their prayer, Dad started chuckling and making comments to his Iranian friends.

Mom stopped the prayer and started yelling at Dad, and the next thing you know, Mom and Dad were arguing in front of everyone. It felt like *My Big Fat Iranian Open-Heart Surgery*!

Wondering what all the commotion was, the nurse came in to find my mom upset.

"I'm getting her out of here. She does not need this kind of stress put on her heart," the nurse said, looking at us as if we were crazy.

Mom and Dad wouldn't even say good-bye to each other as they put Mom on a gurney and prepared her to be taken to the surgical ward.

Nastaran and I decided to walk alongside Mom as she was being pushed down the hallway on the stretcher. We held her hand, trying to say anything but good-bye. As we got to the end of the long hallway, we came to the place where the hallway was separated by two automatic swinging doors. On the other side was the surgical ward. There was a sign on each door that read "Authorized Personnel Only."

I asked the nurse to stop a second so we could pray over our mom one more time. As I prayed, I peeked down the hallway. I could see my father, saying good-bye to his friends, and making his way toward us.

As soon as I said amen, Nastaran looked over to the nurse and pleaded to go through the doors with Mom, so that she could lay hands on the operating room door.

The nurse knew we were not allowed, but seeing the desperation and fear in a daughter's eyes must have melted her heart. She told Nastaran that if she snuck in behind her without anyone seeing, she wouldn't tell.

I was about to ask if I could go as well, when the nurse looked at me and said "just one." I kissed Mom's forehead, inhaling the scent of Trésor. "I'll see you in about seven hours, Mom," and they wheeled her in for surgery.

Thirty minutes had passed, and I was still in the hallway. By this time, Dad was standing by me, not saying a word. We knew there was a waiting room down the hallway, but we couldn't bear to be any further away than we had to be.

I was in a state of perpetual prayer mixed with a few distracting thoughts when I heard the scream.

"No! No!"

The automatic doors busted wide open.

"They lost her! They lost Mom!" Nastaran yelled.

Dad and I stampeded into the forbidden zone and followed my sister.

There was no one in the hallway to kick us out, but it wouldn't have mattered because we were not leaving.

Nastaran was crying and pointing to an unlit red light that was right outside Mom's operating room. "Just pray for that light to stay off. Just pray."

She told us that Mom had flatlined twice during her angiogram.

The little I knew about an angiogram was that this was a test where the doctors inject a colored dye into your heart, and with an X-ray machine they monitor the dye as it flows through the heart. Mom's heart was so weak that as soon as they administered the dye, her heart stopped beating, and her vital signs went flat.

"All I can tell you," she continued, "is when that red light started flashing, everything went crazy. They started shocking Mom to try to get her heart going again. They brought her back, but she's barely alive. Pray the red light doesn't come on again."

I didn't know if she had her facts straight or not, but whatever was happening, this was not good.

I would love to say that I began to pray like crazy, but honestly, I just couldn't think straight. My mom was about to die. How was I going to explain to Benjamin that Mom was not going to be around anymore? All her children loved her, but he needed her more than anybody.

Dad and I paced nervously, while Nastaran stood in place, laying one hand on the door, praying silently.

Ten or fifteen minutes passed with no news or activity. I assumed they were preparing for another angiogram.

"*No!*" Nastaran yelled again.

I turned to find our worst nightmare come true. The red light was on.

My sister was already on her knees, both hands on the door, begging God out loud, "*No God, please no!*"

I fell to the floor as well. Now both of us begged the Lord. "*Please don't take her away! We need her here! Please, Jesus, please!*"

Time was standing still now, and everything was in slow motion. It might have been a second, it may have been hours. I knew I was yelling, and I could see blurrily through my tear-filled eyes that Nastaran was too, but all I could hear was silence.

I felt a hand on my shoulder that brought me back to reality. Dad was beside me, his head on my shoulder, and his knees bent.

"Jesus, please! Jesus, please!" he cried.

At that very instant the red light stopped flashing. We were all reeling from the experience, but no one seemed to have any words at that moment. Nastaran and I were stunned that Dad was kneeling, much less crying out to Jesus.

Two weeks later, Mom was out of the hospital and recovering well.

I had been waiting for the right moment to bring up that traumatic moment when Dad cried out to Jesus.

"Hey Mom, you know the other day when you flatlined and we almost lost you? Guess who was calling out the name of Jesus? Dad was!"

Mom's eyes lit up, and she looked at my father. "You believe in Jesus now?"

"Yes."

"You're going to go to church with us?"

"Yes."

"Hey Dad, are you going to tithe?" I asked, ribbing him.

"No."

We all laughed.

We sat by my mother's bedside and talked to Dad about the gospel—how believing in the power of Jesus was a good place to start, but to truly believe meant to give one's whole self to Christ.

"Dad, are you ready to ask Jesus to forgive your sins and take over?"

"Yes."

16

As for Me and My House . . .

W hat were we thinking? Two weddings in one
weekend?

The idea was insane, but somehow all the
votes were cast in favor of me and my sister both having our
weddings during the first weekend in June of 1994.

It actually made sense for several reasons. In the first place,
both Nastaran and I were engaged, and we both knew that
we planned to get married in the summer. Also, our out-of-
town guests who didn't have the time or the money to travel
to two weddings so close together wouldn't have to pick one

or the other. They could come in for one weekend and make both weddings. As a matter of fact, some who might have declined were now more likely to come since the occasion was twice as grand.

Jennifer and I had originally picked August as the month, but that meant we would be spending the summer away from each other because of my traveling and speaking. I had seven camps and four festivals confirmed on the calendar, and most were being held in vacation-type resorts like the beach or the mountains. Jennifer and I realized that instead of being apart, we could actually go to most of these camps together and turn the summer into a long honeymoon. So the idea of moving the August date to June seemed like the smarter move.

I was also ready to tie the knot for more personal reasons. Just because I was a minister who was marrying a good Christian girl didn't mean we weren't tempted physically. I had made those mistakes before in previous relationships, so I wanted to reduce the risk of doing anything we would regret. Jennifer and I had dated for over two months before our first kiss. It came about a week after her grandmother's funeral. A week after the moment when we first exchanged "I love you's." Now we spent our time talking about where we would live, what furniture to decorate with, and wedding details. The waiting was getting tougher and tougher. We both knew that a shorter engagement would mean a shorter minefield of temptation to walk through.

Everyone was happy about this grand idea except Benjamin, who felt left out because he was the only sibling not

getting married. Ben and I sat and talked about it, but after
I asked him to be my best man at my wedding, he cheered up
and was ready to move forward with the plan. He also appointed the last day of the weekend as Benjamin Nasser Day,
complete with a party for him with all the stayover guests.

After much planning, the weekend schedule was as
follows:

Thurs. 7:00 p.m.: David's and Cary's bachelor parties

Fri. 3:00 p.m.: Jennifer and David's rehearsal at Northport Baptist Church

Fri. 6:00 p.m.: Nastaran and Cary's wedding at the
Birmingham Botanical Gardens

Fri. 7:00 p.m.: An unofficial Iranian wedding ceremony
for both couples

Fri. 8:00 p.m.: Combined wedding rehearsal dinner
and reception at botanical gardens

Sat. 7:00 p.m.: Jennifer and David's wedding at Northport Baptist Church

Sat. 8:00 p.m.: Jennifer and David's reception at Indian
Hills Country Club

Sun.: Benjamin Nasser Day and Jennifer and
David's transatlantic flight to London
for a honeymoon

Throw in airport runs to pick up guests, tuxedo alterations,
and a thousand other last-minute details, and there was simply no margin for error. Everything had to go as planned.

And thankfully all did go as planned, except for one little hitch.

Nastaran and Cary's Friday afternoon wedding went as smoothly as anyone could have imagined. The guests were an eclectic mix: about a hundred Iranian guests, mostly Muslims; a couple hundred American friends and family from all walks of life, many of them Christian; and about twenty-five pastors and youth pastors—almost four hundred guests all together.

Their ceremony was held in the rose garden. The sweet aroma of roses in full bloom filled the air, and someone sang an old Celtic hymn while my sister walked down the aisle to meet her new husband. It rained earlier that day and then the sun made its appearance, so everything was crisp and sparkly.

Afterward, everyone walked over to Dad's restaurant, which was located in the main building at the gardens. As we entered Café de France, we could see that Dad had spared no expense. There were silver chafing dishes filled to the brim with buttery shrimp, filet mignon, and all manner of luxurious food. Two ice sculptures of intertwining swans greeted guests, and a professional harpist played music in the background. Rick Stanley, who was there to officiate our wedding the next day, looked over at me. "This is the kind of party Elvis would have thrown, Bud."

Before the reception began, the plan was to have a brief Iranian civil ceremony in the rotunda room. But by the time it was all said and done, there was nothing "civil" about it.

Mom and Dad had asked both couples if it would be okay to have an unofficial Iranian ceremony in the midst of the weekend. In an effort to honor their Middle Eastern heritage, and out of respect for their friends and family, they wanted to make room for some Persian influence.

Much like the unity candle, or the father giving away the bride in a Western wedding, Iranians have symbolic gestures and actions in their weddings as well. During the actual ceremony, the bride and groom sit, while women hold a silk canopy above their heads. Large sugar cones are rubbed together over the canopy, resulting in a shower of sweetness over the newlyweds. While the sugar is falling on the canopy, other women are sewing seven strands of colored threads to sew up the mother-in-law's tongue— only figuratively, of course! A *sofreh-ye aqd* (an intricate hand-sewn wedding cloth), is spread out, covered with many objects traditionally associated with a happy and fruitful marriage, as well as bowls and plates piled with nuts, fruits, and delicious Persian sweets. In keeping with Persian tradition, we all agreed to this type of celebration, thinking it could be really special.

The only thing that all four of us were absolutely adamant about was that whoever performed the ceremony couldn't have anything Muslim said or read. This was to be a celebration of culture rather than religion.

As we got to the rotunda room, I saw a long-bearded man dressed in an embroidered *kurta* and a *taqiyah* prayer cap. My father was standing next to him, talking. It was obvious he was there for the ceremony. I knew my parents had asked someone to come and officiate, and I figured he would be Muslim, but I had no idea he would be a mullah.

This man was obviously Islamic clergy.

I walked over to introduce myself, but also to make sure he knew that we wanted nothing Islamic in the ceremony.

I asked if Dad had made it clear that both couples were committed Christians, and he nodded yes.

Nastaran and Cary went first. Fresh out of their actual wedding, they came and sat under the canopy, and the ceremony began. For an instant, it felt as though we were back in Iran. Dark-haired, olive-skinned women performed their ceremonial duties, while a man with a thick Middle Eastern accent addressed the crowd.

The mullah's words were hard to understand, but in his broken English he made a few predictable statements about the beauty of marriage and the reasons to celebrate it. Then he looked at my new brother-in-law and said, "Cary, you have been given this woman by Allah to lead. Do you take her hand and promise to lead her in service to Allah according to his teachings in the Qu'ran?"

Cary turned beet red and looked at Nastaran in shock.

The mullah repeated it again, but Cary did not say anything.

The mullah then turned to my sister and asked her basically the same question. Nastaran just smiled and remained silent. A few more moments and the mullah, obviously irritated, said a few closing words and finished.

Cary and my sister's silent protest flooded the room with tension. The room was filled with Muslims, preachers, nominally religious people, and everything in between. One can only imagine the diversity of thoughts that filled the minds of that crowd.

But I did not have to guess what my future father-in-law was thinking.

Mr. Davis said to Jennifer, "I don't like this. I don't like this at all."

I understood where he was coming from. He wanted the best for his daughter—a man who loved God and loved her—but the mullah represented a different god, a different world, and a different life than the one he wanted for Jennifer.

It was our turn.

I grabbed Jennifer's hand, looked Mr. Davis right in the eyes and said, "Sir, you have to trust me."

As we walked over to sit, I whispered to Jennifer, "Just follow me, Baby, don't be nervous."

We sat under the canopy, waiting for the mullah to escape the wrath of my mother, who had cornered him to remind him of his promise to keep things civil and not religious.

The mullah walked back and faced Jennifer and me, ready to begin.

This time he skipped the pleasantries.

With a smile that suppressed his anger he said, "You have only one way for your marriage to be blessed by Allah. David, do you take Jennifer's hand and promise to lead her in service to Allah according to his teachings in the Qu'ran?"

"I do . . . take her hand, but as for me and my house, we will serve the Lord. His name is Jesus Christ, and he is the way, the truth, and the life. No one can come to the Father, except through him." I said this loud enough for everyone to hear.

But then the best part of all happened.

Jennifer—quiet, shy, hates-to-talk-in-front-of-a-crowd Jennifer—piped up and said, "We will live our lives based on the teachings of the Holy Bible . . . sir."

I never loved her more than in that moment.

Hand-in-hand, we were letting all the world know that we had escaped religion for the God of grace, and our life together was going to be about blessing the one who set us free.

As we stood up, Iranian men began to throw gold coins at us, representing hope for prosperity, and women came over to Jennifer to crown her with jewelry that they had brought over from Iran.

I walked over to Mr. Davis, and before I could say a word, he smiled and hugged my neck.

"I trust you" is all he said.

Twenty-four hours later, Mr. Davis proved his trust as he escorted his little girl down the same aisle he had walked thirty years before on his own wedding day. No woman in all of history had ever looked more stunning than my new wife.

I looked down at the front row and saw my family. They were *all* my family. The Davises on one side, and the Nassers on the other. But they were more than fathers and mothers; they were my brothers and sisters in Christ.

During the wedding Rick Stanley, my mentor and friend, shared the gospel and explained that marriage is nothing more than a reflection of who we are as Christians, the bride of Christ.

The next day Jennifer and I sat on a plane ready to cross the ocean for our honeymoon in London. As we listened to the pilot say that we had perfect visibility, not a cloud in the sky, my mind went back all those years when I was on a plane heading out of Iran. Instead of my dad's hand, however, I was holding the hand of the love of my life. I felt the same sense of security with her that I had felt while gripping tightly to my father, even when, on both occasions, the future was uncertain. Ironically, the greatest difference in this plane ride into the unknown, and the one that had happened fifteen years before, was not that one was an escape and another was a homecoming of sorts. Nor was it that I was once jumping out of a war zone and now I was diving headfirst into a great love affair. Nor was it that while I once held confidence in my father, now my confidence rested in my wife. No. While both plane rides were heading toward unpredictabilty, the greatest difference, now as then, lay in the fact that while I didn't know what the future would hold for me, I did know the one who held my future. My security, for once in my life, lay not in a country, a political agenda, a set of circumstances, a social standing, nor even in an individual. It lay solely, completely in the hands of God. My relationship with Jesus Christ gave me a firm foundation in which my future was embedded. I could face whatever the future held with peace instead of fear. More important than the hand I gripped to help me through the fires was the hand in which we were both resting.

Epilogue

I find it sweetly ironic that I am sitting at the kitchen table writing the last pages of this book at 10:37 p.m., on the evening of Red Wednesday, 2009. This was not planned by me, but orchestrated by a God who is using the writing of this memoir as a vehicle to reveal his perfect timing in all things. This is *chaharshambe soori*, when Middle Easterners celebrate the burning away of misery and pain, and the rising up of great promise for the future. My heart is filled with joy as I write these final thoughts. What a great night we've just had.

Everyone arrived around six o'clock, dressed in red, ready for good fellowship, good food, and good old-fashioned pyromania.

My kitchen still smells like *mahi doodi*, intensely smoked cod that had to be ordered from the Iranian produce market.

Nastaran and I skinned and prepared it before our twenty-seven guests arrived, so my fingers have the same smell, despite several attempts to wash the odor away. Maybe Clorox will do the job.

The fish was accompanied by several less daring options for the Western guests who would join us tonight. There were four different types of basmati rice. There was chicken marinated in saffron, olive oil, and lemon juice. Then there was Jennifer's favorite Iranian dish, *kokoo sabzi*, a vegetable soufflé made with parsley, dill, coriander, spring onions, barberries, and chopped walnuts. These delicacies and more filled platters on the very table that has become my writing desk. Now, instead of food, two laptops sit side by side, both on and in use. One is mine, on which I'm typing; the other is Jennifer's. She is downloading pictures taken earlier tonight with her camera. We took a lot of them. This was a night well worth remembering.

We took dozens of pictures of the piles of sticks and hay burning upward of five feet as our guests and family ran straight through the flames. Some with fear in their eyes, but most with childlike wonder. We had all sorts here, from veteran fire jumpers who grew up in Iran, to American guests who had no idea what to expect. The first-timers picked a good year to participate, because after nearly thirty years of celebrating Red Wednesday in the States, we finally found the ideal location. No more scaring the neighbors, no more embarrassing stares, no more fears that someone is going to call the fire department. This year, the event was held at my house, on eight secluded acres, where a clan of crimson-outfitted Persians can cause all the commotion they want.

A few pictures from tonight are particularly meaningful to me.

For instance, there is my daughter, Grace, playing dress up with her cousin and best friend, Simine. One glance and it becomes obvious who belongs to whom. Simene is the spitting image of Nastaran, her mother, and Grace looks like a hybrid of Jennifer and me. Her curly, thick hair and long eyelashes are passed down from her daddy, but luckily she has her mother's nose and amazing smile. (Trust me, the more she looks like Jennifer, the better.) Grace is full of life and energy, but she possesses compassion and mercy in no small measure.

Or there's this one—the picture of my son, Rudy, playing Ping-Pong in the garage against his cousin Emmanuel. As an eleven-year-old, Rudy is the older brother of his seven-year-old sister, but he wasn't our first child. God gave Grace a big brother from Guatemala when she was two-and-a-half years old. We adopted Rudy in 2004. The twenty-one months it took to bring him home was a difficult time, but well worth it. Rudy is winsome, tender-hearted, funny—but best of all, a man of God.

Perhaps my favorite is the picture of my mom and dad jumping through the fire together, Mom wearing a red leather Armani jacket, and Dad, a cashmere sweater—in seventy-degree weather. Not exactly what I would have chosen to wear on such an occasion, but precisely what I would have guessed they would wear. Dad is retired now. Having sold the restaurant last year, he spends his time at home with Benjamin and my mother. They fill their days figuring out ways to spoil their grandkids. Benjamin works part-time at a Christian bookstore as a greeter, and Mom has started a Persian-language Bible study that meets weekly. Dad helps out his church, doing hospital visitations with one of the senior pastors.

Watching these pictures download reminds me of a million other moments in the past. I realize now that whether I saw it or not, God has always been the central figure in every picture. I see him now, holding us through every single frame of our life in his righteous right hand. And his unceasing presence in our yesterdays is our hope and assurance for the fires of our tomorrows.

ACKNOWLEDGMENTS

The book you're holding in your hand is the result of a team effort. I realize my name is the only one you see on the cover, but without the countless hours of hard work by a great group of people, *Jumping through Fires* would be nothing more than a handful of memories roaming around in my head.

I'd like to thank John Perry for the tremendous amount of help in writing this book; the entire team at Creative Trust for representing this project with such excellence; the Baker Publishing family for believing in me as an author; my family and friends for prayer and support; and, last but not least, Jesus Christ for turning tragedy into testimony. May this book bring you honor and glory.

Glory Revealed: The Word of God in Worship is a ten song, Scripture-driven worship project. The songs on this CD are the passages inspired from *Glory Revealed*, the book.

Glory Revealed returns with another powerful, Scripture-driven worship project: *Glory Revealed II: The Word of God in Worship*

Albums featuring recordings by:

Trevor Morgan, Third Day's Mac Powell, Steven Curtis Chapman, Brian Littrell, David Crowder, Shane & Shane, Josh Bates, Michael W. Smith, Starfield's Tim Neufeld, Casting Crown's Mark Hall, Amy Grant, Sarah Evans, Ed Cash, Kari Jobe and Matt Maher.

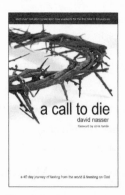

This 40-day journey explores what it means to die to self daily, so that Christ can live in and through us.

A 20-chapter exposition discovering how the invisible God makes himself known. See His glory revealed.

Available now in bookstores.

A 39-day look at how the grace-filled life is not about doing but about being. New look, same Scripture-based message.

A four-session Bible study for teens on what a real relationship with God looks like. David Nasser will offer hope and encouragement to teens from Scripture on their winding journey of faith.

If you could ask God one question, what would it be? How can God love me when I've done so much wrong? How do I know God is speaking to me? How can God be real and ignore all the bad things that happen? Teens are struggling with very difficult questions and doubts.

Four sessions with insightful topics:
Looking for God, When Bad Things Happen, Identity, Questions of Faith

Includes: 2 DVDs • 60-page Leader's Guide • Reproducible handouts for the group

Has anything really changed in 2000 years?
Students in America are growing up in a culture that places high emphasis on entertainment, politics and self. It's increasingly difficult for Scriptural Truth to cut through the noise and sink into the hearts and minds of this next generation.

In these four sessions, David Nasser uses the life of Paul to highlight how followers of Christ can stand up to cultural "norms" and stand firm in Christ.

Four video-driven sessions with insightful topics:
1.) Culture & Faith in Conflict (8 minutes)   3.) Keep the Faith (10 minutes)
2.) Not Good Enough? (13 minutes)   4.) A Picture of Your Life (9 minutes)

Includes: 2 DVDs • 60-page Leader's Guide • Reproducible handouts for the group

Available from D. Nasser Outreach*
For more information call 205-982-9996 or visit www.davidnasser.com.
*Not available in stores.